SCHOOL DEVELOPMENT SERIES

General Editors: David Hopkins and David Reynolds

THE EMPOWERED SCHOOL

THE EMPOWERED SCHOOL
The management and practice of development planning

David H. Hargreaves
David Hopkins

with the assistance of
Marilyn Leask

continuum
LONDON • NEW YORK

Continuum
The Tower Building
11 York Road
London SE1 7NX

First published 1991
Reprinted 1992 (twice), 1993, 1994, 1996, 1998, 2003
This edition 2005

British Library Cataloguing-in-Publication Data
Hargreaves, David H. (David Harold) *1939–*
    The empowered school: the management and practice of development planning.
    I. Schools. Management
    I. Title   II. Hopkins, David *1949–*   III. Leask, Marilyn
    371.2

ISBN 0-8264-7762-3

Typeset by Fakenham Photosetting Limited, Fakenham, Norfolk

Printed and bound in Great Britain by the Cromwell Press, Trowbridge, Wiltshire

Contents

Preface

The best-known outcome of the School Development Plans project is the booklet *Planning for School Development*, copies of which were issued by the Department of Education and Science to Local Education Authorities for distribution to schools in spring 1990. The project team also prepared two notes of advice for LEA officers. In July 1990 the final report of the project was submitted to the DES.

This book is a compilation of these four documents, which remain Crown copyright, together with some additional material and ideas. Some LEAs have issued guidelines on school development planning and many individual schools have evolved their own approach. This book is designed to complement such existing work as well as to provide a comprehensive account for all those who wish to understand what is involved and who may be thinking about devising a scheme for development planning.

It is intended as a practical guide to action. The audience we have in mind is anyone who may be involved in development planning, but especially headteachers, teachers, governors and LEA officers (a term we use to include advisers and inspectors).

Part 1 (Chapters 1–3) describes school development planning and provides a rationale for it. The management of development planning and how this relates to the management of schools is also discussed, since we believe that effective development planning often requires some re-conceptualization of school management.

Part 2 (Chapters 4–10) is a step-by-step guide to the process of development planning, beginning with the initial steps of preparation and concluding with a portrayal of what happens to a school when all involved acquire some experience of development planning.

Part 3 (Chapters 11–13) explores the partnership between schools and LEAs which supports successful development planning, and includes advice for when things go wrong.

Part 4 (Chapter 14), the only chapter with an academic focus, relates development planning to some aspects of the literature on school effectiveness and school improvement.

Part 5 is a resource file in which detailed guidance is provided on topics which underpin development planning. These files have been designed so that they can be used as a resource for meetings, discussions and activities on appropriate occasions, such as a professional training day.

We would not have undertaken the programme of research and development were we not convinced that development planning has a very important role to play in the tasks of managing change and school improvement.

Development planning is still, however, in its infancy and there remains much to be learnt. We have drawn freely upon the experiences of all who were involved with the project. We do not present any case-studies in the usual sense of that term. We think it more helpful to draw out from a wide range of practices adopted by different schools and LEAs what seem to us both to be the key principles which lie behind the most effective practice and to be some of the dangers which need to be avoided.

It is the nature of development planning that it is not a simple set of practices, techniques or recipes that one school can copy from another. Every school has to find its own unique approach to development planning; this is essential if there is to be real progress in making the school a more effective and rewarding place for teachers and students.

The way this comes about is best described as a process of *empowerment*. The empowered school is neither the unwilling victim of externally driven changes nor the innovator who reacts unthinkingly to every fad or whim. It is the school which responds to the challenge of change by recreating its own vision, by redefining management to support change and by releasing the energy and confidence to put its ideas into practice.

We have come to the firm conclusion that development planning is not just one more fashionable idea or yet another innovation of temporary relevance in turbulent times. It is a means rather than an end, a path rather than a destination. Development planning is characterized by empowerment when it succeeds; but it also generates an empowerment which endures above and beyond any particular changes that are planned and implemented. The most potent guide to development planning is this search for empowerment. We hope this book will make its discovery more enjoyable and a little easier.

David H. Hargreaves, David Hopkins,
Cambridge, January 1991

Acknowledgements

This book is a direct result of our work on the School Development Plans project funded by the Department of Education and Science from April 1989 to August 1990. We are grateful to the DES for so readily agreeing to our proposal for the project and for issuing the project's first booklet, *Planning for School Development*, to LEAs for distribution to all schools in England and Wales. The views expressed in this book, however, are our own and are not necessarily those of the Secretary of State for Education and Science, Local Education Authorities or schools which participated in the project.

We were fortunate in having Marilyn Leask as our research assistant for the duration of the project. She participated fully in all aspects of the research and contributed significantly to the development of the ideas contained in this book. We were also fortunate in being able to enlist the collaboration of Joe Connelly (general adviser, Sussex LEA) and Paul Robinson (at the time education officer in Cambridge LEA and now with Essex LEA) for the first phase of the project. Thanks are also due to Hazel Mander who provided secretarial support and Martin Hodge who helped enormously with word-processing.

Without the co-operation of the schools and LEAs involved in both phases of the project we would not have been able to do our work. We are extremely grateful to the teachers, headteachers, governors and LEA officers who courteously gave of their time and shared their experiences with us.

For their collaboration and help during the first phase of the project, we wish to thank many LEAs and schools which provided access to their development planning documents. Thanks are also due to a number of governors and members of the National Association of Governors and Managers.

We are grateful to the following for their co-operation with the second phase of the project:

Acton Green Combined School, Ealing
Arnside National C of E School, Cumbria
Backworth First School, North Tyneside
Burnside Community High School, North Tyneside
Burntmill Comprehensive School, Essex
Chace School, Enfield
Christchurch Infants School, Redbridge
Ellen Wilkinson High School, Ealing
Feniton C of E Primary School, Devon
The Groves High School, Clwyd

Hatton School for Children with Learning Difficulties, Redbridge
Heybridge Primary School, Essex
Honilands Primary School, Enfield
Icknield High School, Bedfordshire
Lydgate Middle School, Sheffield
Monks Orchard Primary School, Croydon
Norham High School, North Tyneside
Penyffordd County Primary School, Clwyd
St Joseph's College, Croydon
St Mary and St Margaret C of E Junior and Infant School, Solihull
Settlebeck High School, Cumbria
Smith's Wood School, Solihull
Stewartby Middle School, Bedfordshire
Teign School, Devon
Whirlow Brook School, Sheffield

Julia Bell,	Primary Inspector,	North Tyneside
Alan Brown,	Headteacher,	Bedfordshire (now with Buckinghamshire)
Jackie Calcroft,	Headteacher,	Ealing
David Curtis,	Senior Inspector,	Solihull
Martin Gazzard,	Schools Officer,	Sheffield
Carol Jones,	Primary Inspector,	Croydon (now with Surrey)
Howard Morrall,	INSET Co-ordinator,	Redbridge
Geoff Rate,	Headteacher,	Clwyd
Paul Robinson,	Education Officer (Schools),	Essex
Ian Terrell,	Advisory Teacher,	Enfield
Geoff Thomas,	Headteacher,	Devon
Carol Tiddy,	General Inspector,	Cumbria

PART ONE

CONTEXT

Chapter 1

What is a School Development Plan?

The purpose of development planning is to improve the quality of teaching and learning in a school through the successful management of innovation and change.

Development planning encourages governors, heads and staff (teachers and support staff) to ask four basic questions:

- Where is the school now?

- What changes do we need to make?

- How shall we manage these changes over time?

- How shall we know whether our management of change has been successful?

Development planning helps the school to provide practical answers to these questions. This will, of course, itself take time and energy: the gain is that the school is enabled *to organize what it is already doing and what it needs to do in a more purposeful and coherent way*.

The distinctive feature of a development plan is that it brings together, *in an overall plan*, national and LEA policies and initiatives, the school's aim and values, its existing achievements and its needs for development. By co-ordinating aspects of planning which are otherwise separate, the school acquires a shared sense of direction and is able to control and manage the tasks of development and change. A development plan is easily described. Priorities for development are selected and planned in detail for one year and are supported by action plans or working documents for staff. The priorities for later years are sketched in outline to provide the longer-term programme.

Development *planning* is more than a development *plan*, the document: it is the *process* of creating the plan and then ensuring that it is put into effect. The plan is a statement of intentions which reflect the school's vision for the future. The process involves reaching agreement on a sensible set of priorities for the school and then taking action to realize the plan.

When a school embarks on development planning for the first time, attention is focused on the plan rather than the process of planning. People ask questions such as: What does a plan look like? What sort of document is it? What makes a development plan a *good* plan? Can you show us a plan to guide our own thinking?

These are reasonable and understandable questions. Although they are the ones that first spring to mind, they are not the best place to begin (and in practice schools find it much easier than they imagine to write a plan as a document).

An understanding of the process of development planning is the key to success. The production of a good plan and its successful implementation depend upon a sound grasp of the processes involved. A wise choice of content for the plan as well as means of implementing the plan successf 'ly will be made only when the process of development planning is thoroughly understood.

There are four main processes in development planning (see Figure 1.1):

- *audit*: a school reviews its strengths and weaknesses;
- *construction*: priorities for development are selected and then turned into specific targets;
- *implementation*: the planned priorities and targets are implemented;
- *evaluation*: the success of implementation is checked.

Getting started (see Chapter 4) is also an important part of the process. It is always a mistake to rush into development planning: making the right preparations is worth the time and effort involved.

The terms for these processes vary between schools and LEAs. For convenience, we have chosen these particular working headings, but each school and LEA may prefer different names for what are essentially the same processes.

The more important point is that these processes should be viewed in a holistic way. They should not be seen as discrete stages, but as processes or phases that fuse into and inform one another. A common error, painfully learnt in some schools, is to tackle each process as an independent stage, embarking on one process with little consideration of the full implications for what is to follow. From the beginning the school must have a grasp of the whole, the total process of development planning, and it is not just the head and senior staff who need to adopt this holistic perspective.

The rest of Part 1 of this book is designed to help governors, heads and staff to take this holistic view and to think through the vitally important stage of preparing for development planning.

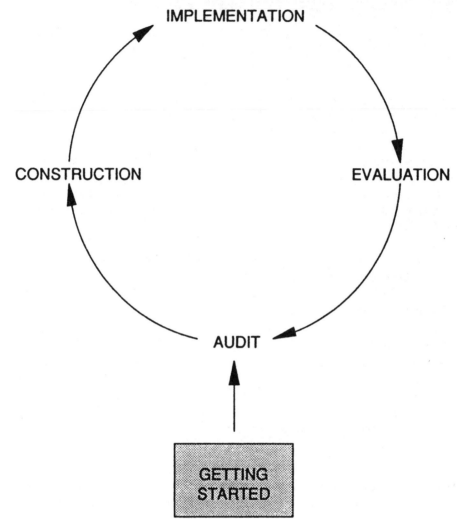

Figure 1.1 *The development planning cycle*

Chapter 2

Why School Development Plans?

'School development plans? Not another initiative!' We have heard this response from many hard-pressed governors, heads and teachers who have come to see any new initiative as just one more demand upon their time and energy – the straw that threatens to break the camel's back.

There is some justification in this reaction. Everyone involved with schools is already so overwhelmed with change that there is little time for anything else. The test must be whether development planning will be worth the time and energy involved and whether it will help the school to be more successful in managing the changes which it has already accepted it has to undertake.

Development planning is designed to allow the school to organize, with greater efficiency and success, its existing programme of development and change. Because it promises greater control over the ubiquitous problem of 'innovation overload' with greater success in making the changes actually work, development planning is worth serious consideration.

ADVANTAGES OF DEVELOPMENT PLANNING

Heads and teachers with whom we have spoken felt that there were eight main advantages:

- A development plan focuses attention on the aims of education, especially the learning and achievement, broadly defined, of all pupils.

- A development plan provides a comprehensive and co-ordinated approach to all aspects of planning, one which covers curriculum and assessment, teaching, management and organization, finance and resources.

- The development plan captures the long-term vision for the school within which manageable short-term goals are set. The priorities contained in the plan represent the school's translation of policy into its agenda for action.

- A development plan helps to relieve the stress on teachers caused by the pace of change. Teachers come to exercise greater control over change rather than feeling controlled by it.

- The achievements of teachers in promoting innovation and change receive wider recognition, so that their confidence rises.

- The quality of staff development improves. In-service training and appraisal help the school to work more effectively and help teachers to acquire new knowledge and skills as part of their professional development.

- The partnership between the teaching staff and the governing body is strengthened.

- The task of reporting on the work of the school is made easier.

Probably the main reason why schools and LEAs have taken up development planning in recent years is that it offers a means of managing rapid and substantial change. But this is not, in the most successful schools, the primary *benefit* of development planning. The principal gain is that it allows the school to focus on its fundamental aims concerned with teaching and learning. Development planning is really about school and classroom improvement. Many of the current changes with which schools have to cope are being imposed from outside. Development planning is the way in which each school interprets external policy requirements so that they are integrated into its own unique life and culture.

Teachers are more accountable than in the past to governors and parents. This is easily seen as threatening, a crude 'calling to account'. Development planning creates a partnership between teachers, governors, parents, LEA officers and others in which there is a shared commitment to the school's improvement, and a shared responsibility for the school's progress and success in achieving such improvement. This partnership of mutual support and accountability is one of the major underlying themes of this book, for it is a prerequisite of effective development planning and school improvement.

Although the governors formally approve a development plan and they, along with many of the school's partners, are involved with implementing the plan, most of the work involved will fall upon classroom teachers. They will be motivated by and committed to the plan when:

- they make a personal and professional gain from the activities required by the plan, i.e. they believe that the plan will help them to be more effective and more fulfilled;

- the impact of the plan will be an improvement in the quality of teaching and learning in classrooms;

- they believe that the time and effort required of them are reasonable.

Governors and heads need to bear this in mind when the development plan is being constructed. Effective development planning requires everyone involved to have a real stake in it: all must recognize the advantages and pay-off for them as well as for the school as a whole.

7

DEVELOPMENT PLANNING AND THE FALLACIES OF CHANGE

When a school chooses to engage in development planning, it is not merely recognizing the potential advantage of so doing, but rejecting alternative approaches to change
and improvement in schools. School development planning is still in its infancy: it has
yet to be shown conclusively that this is the best available approach. But it is almost
certainly better than some other approaches, which are now somewhat discredited.
We feel justified in describing these as illusions.

Illusion 1: If the Ripples are not Reaching the Shore, Throw More Stones

Recently there has been considerable debate about whether or not 'standards' of
education in school have fallen. There is, of course, insufficient evidence to substan-
tiate either argument. In any event, the more important question is about how present
standards, whatever they may be, can be raised. When education is high on the
political agenda, and when politicians, both local and national and of all political
persuasions, are committed to raising standards, there is an inevitable impatience with
the rate at which standards can be improved. If one change does not seem to have the
desired effect, the temptation is to introduce further innovations. From the teachers'
point of view, this can produce a paralysis: they become exhausted and demoralized
by trying to do too much too quickly, but with nothing done properly. Moreover,
when they feel bombarded by externally imposed innovations which sometimes arrive
or involve change in unpredictable ways, teachers feel no 'ownership' of or commitment to the innovations.

Development planning increases the school's control over the content and pace of
change. It provides a rationale either for saying 'no' to certain demands, since not
everything can be put into a single year's development plan, or for saying 'not yet',
since some changes are sensibly placed in the second, third or even later years of the
plan. In other words, a strategic approach to planning is adopted and the school ceases
to be a target of demands for instant change.

Illusion 2: Schools are Rational Organizations

Virtually all attempts at educational reform are based on a rational argument and view
of change. Yet in the real world of schools the reforms fail to work as expected. Some
commentators see schools as being 'non-rational'. This is not meant to suggest that
heads and teachers are irrational people, but rather to indicate that schools are very
complex organizations embedded in a disorderly environment of multiple and often
conflicting pressures and expectations. Reformers often take a simplistic view of
change: they pick out a single weakness which they hope to cure by a single change. In
reality both a weakness and a change designed to cure it interact with all the other
factors that contribute to a school's character – strengths and weaknesses included.

Development planning acknowledges the subtle nature of change in schools. As
we hope to show, a development plan cannot be a rag-bag of separate reforms, each of
which is a neat answer to a problem taken out of its institutional context. Development planning begins with the school as a whole, its culture and the way it is
managed. To begin anywhere else is to fall prey to simplistic models of school
improvement and to court failure in educational reform.

Illusion 3: Educational Change is a Systematic Process that Makes a Difference

Unfortunately this is rarely the case. All too often educational change proceeds in fits and starts. Various fads and fashions become popular, are taken up and then replaced. Educational changes are rarely thought through in advance, systematically planned and implemented, then tested and evaluated before wider dissemination. Commonly, what seem to be good ideas are adopted, partially implemented and poorly evaluated, until interest dwindles and another idea comes along.

Development planning offers a genuinely more systematic and sustained approach – a more careful selection of a limited range of priorities, better planning with the support of pre-defined resources and staff development, and more thorough evaluation to establish new strengths on which to build over time.

Illusion 4: Once the Policy is Passed, then Implementation will Proceed on Autopilot

Creating a new policy – at the national, LEA or school levels – is never more than the first and easiest step in the change process. Our educational history is littered with examples of good policies that were never put into practice because reformers thought that the formulation of the policy was the most important part of change, and that if it was not successfully implemented then someone (the teachers?) should be blamed for 'obstructing' the policy.

Development planning emphasizes the whole process of change, from defining the need for and value of policy, through its formulation, to its implementation and evaluation. The whole process needs care and attention. But it is not a mechanical process. It will not proceed as planned. There will be obstacles and diversions; some changes will need to be made *en route*; some outcomes will not be achieved in full, but there will also be unintended outcomes and benefits.

Development planning assumes change is an organic process of growth. Not all the parts grow at the same time or at the same rate; but the parts are interconnected, and growth in one part affects and is affected by the other parts. Organic growth involves a change in the shape and functioning of the whole. Too often in the past schools have made innovations in isolated parts of their work, resulting in temporary and superficial change. When a school acknowledges its own organic character, it has established a basis for development planning in which the school's culture and its overall approach to the management of its affairs support the changes it seeks to make and in turn are themselves changed through a shared endeavour and collective learning.

Development planning, in short, focuses on:

- the school's culture, management and organization as a whole;
- its policies and practices for teaching and learning for all teachers and all pupils;
- the outcomes and pay-off for teachers and pupils.

BUILDING ON THE PAST

Development planning is not so new as the name might suggest. Schools have always planned their work, and the four main processes we have described – audit, construction, implementation and evaluation – are already alive in every school. It is simply that in recent years schools and LEAs have, under the pressure for change, given more thought to how the planning and management of change need to be more self-conscious and deliberate. Sometimes this sprang from schemes of school self-evaluation or school-based review, by which the teaching staff, usually in association with LEA officers, examine in a systematic way the strengths and weaknesses of the school. Much has been learnt from these schemes, but for most schools it has proved to be easier to identify priorities for future development than to implement selected targets within a specific time frame. School self-evaluation has consequently had limited effects on the daily life of most schools.

A number of related developments have further helped some schools to develop skills in planning. Schemes of financial delegation operated by a few LEAs have led schools to consider more fully the financial implications of their forward planning; and the advent of the LEA Training Grants Scheme improved the capacity of both LEAs and schools to plan INSET provision and its evaluation in relation to identified needs and specific areas for development. In other words, a financial plan and an INSET or staff development plan have begun to emerge in embryonic form.

Schools involved in the Technical and Vocational Education Initiative (TVEI) and its extension have learnt much about curricular planning and how it is resourced in terms of staffing as well as materials and equipment. Schools which have piloted various schemes of staff appraisal have discovered that real professional development usually requires changes to management and planning.

Such developments, often with distinctive origins and different time-scales, overlap and interconnect. Development planning brings them together in an explicit way, using them as springboards to a more holistic approach to planning.

As the whole process of planning becomes integrated, it permeates the normal work of the school. Planning is no longer a set of specialized or independent activities, but a process which encompasses the more routine activities. In other words, system maintenance (or operational activities) is more closely linked to system development (or strategic activities). This can be expressed diagrammatically as in the school development cone (see Figure 2.1), where planning becomes more coherent as it is assimilated into the daily life of the school and is related to the school's major aim of pupil achievement.

This is a tall order for many schools. But although each school and each LEA has to acquire the skills for this work in their own ways and will create their own, rightly unique, versions of development, they do not need to re-invent the wheel of development planning from scratch. The schools and LEAs which pioneered development planning can, from their own hard-won experience, offer some guidance to other schools, who turn to the idea with a mixture of enthusiasm, anxiety and lack of confidence.

Schools which are most successful with development planning have found ways of avoiding the following dangers:

- Development planning is treated like many new developments with

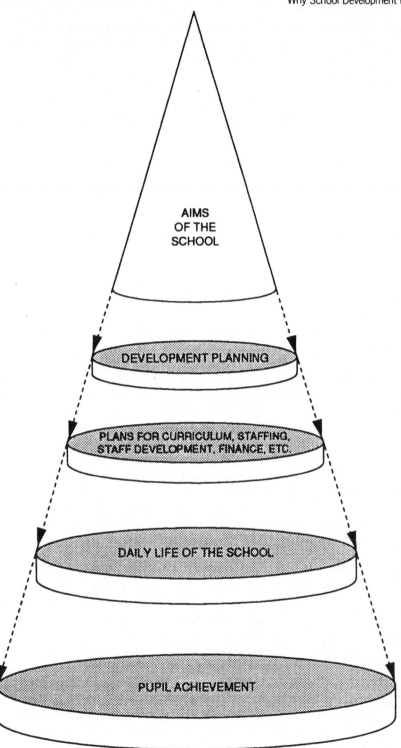

Figure 2.1 *The development planning cone*

which schools have to cope and is 'bolted on' to the existing work of the school as a kind of extra, but does not change in any fundamental way how the school manages itself.

- The school underestimates the extent to which development planning has to be managed and does not realize that this may require significant changes to the way the school has been managed in the past.

- There is a lack of recognition of the special character of development planning, the purpose of which is to create the conditions under which a school will find it easier to implement all the other changes and innovations that it needs to make.

- The school produces a development plan as a written document but gives insufficient attention to the process of development planning.

LOOKING TO THE FUTURE

Attention to these lessons will help a school to be successful with its very first development plan. And it is important that this first plan should be as successful as possible, since this inspires confidence, readiness to learn, and real achievements on which to build. The governors and head need to take care that the first experience of development planning is rewarding for all who are involved. If the preparations are inadequate, the plan fails. In these cases, it is not merely that (yet) another innovation fails: it is that the school's capacity for all future innovation may well be further weakened by its initial lack of success with development planning.

The LEA has a key role. We have seen some excellent examples of LEA guidelines on development planning, and these are generally welcomed by schools. But where the LEA makes development planning mandatory, where schools are given a short time to prepare the development plan, and where the officers are themselves insufficiently trained in the complexities of development planning to give the necessary support to schools, relationships between schools and officers become strained. What has been offered by LEAs to schools as a help can soon become a hindrance. The role of LEA officers is subject to rapid change as they forge new relationships with schools. We believe that with the right partnership between officers and schools, development planning will be more effective. Throughout Part 2 of this book, which describes the processes in detail, we make reference to the work of LEA officers at appropriate points. Part 3 discusses the partnership between schools and officers in a more specific and systematic way.

Our main focus in Part 1 is on the school itself and the changing relationships within it. The effects of the Education Reform Act (1988) and other recent legislation are slowly making their impact. As schemes of the local management of schools (LMS) are implemented and responsibility for budgets is delegated, governors and heads are coping with financial matters that are often new and sometimes alien to them. Our view is that most governors and heads will gain confidence and skill in these matters quite quickly – and far sooner than they think. LMS really is as much about *management* as it is about *finance*, which is why the term was coined in preference to local financial management. We believe that when heads and governors see LMS as a spur to development planning (of which financial management is a component), they have taken a road to what will truly be 'self-managing schools' – ones which not merely learn to manage change and finance but also learn the art of school improvement which leads to more effective teaching and learning.

Chapter 3

Development Planning and the Management of the School

This is in some ways the most difficult chapter in the book. We suggest that heads and senior staff read it now, then use the ideas discussed here as a lens to bring some features of the chapters in Part 2 into sharper relief. Other readers may prefer to move immediately to Part 2, returning to this chapter after reading Chapter 10. Everyone should read the present chapter at some point.

We have already pointed out that a common motive for interest in development planning is that it offers a systematic approach to the management of change. When, as now, the school is faced with a range of substantial changes at the same time, there is a challenge to the way the school has been managed in past and less hectic times. The school discovers that changes cannot be managed independently of the general or routine management of the school – the discredited 'bolt-on' view of change. Development planning in most schools calls for some rethinking about management as a whole so that the management of change can become *integral* to the way the school conducts its affairs. The school should ideally reach a point where change is not something extra or unusual, but a task with which it can cope comfortably because innovation and change have become a natural part of school management.

Development planning is about the management of change, certainly; but it is also about how the school has to re-create its management so that the *capacity* to manage change is increased. To put the point succinctly, *managing change involves changing management*. The rest of this chapter explores this key idea.

WHAT IS MANAGEMENT?

Textbooks frequently define management as the structures and procedures required to co-ordinate the diverse activities of an organization. The school, like any complex organization, has to create systems for:

- allocating roles and responsibilities;

- making decisions;

- consultation;

- communication (both within the school and with the school's partners);

- allocating resources;

- locating work activities in particular places;

- distributing time to various activities;

14

- monitoring the work of the organization's members.

But if one asks *teachers* this basic question of 'what is management?', most will think not so much in terms of the formal definition given above but of *people* – the head, deputies and senior staff who are often referred to as 'management' or 'senior management'. People rather than structures and procedures spring to mind. It is the job of 'senior management' to manage; that, after all, is what they are paid to do, and leaves teachers free to do what they are supposed to do – *teach*. This reflects the hierarchical structure of staff relations: managers manage and teachers teach. Many teachers are ambivalent about the fact that promotion to a higher salary, status and responsibility entails a reduction in teaching duties.

At the heart of this allocation of roles and division of labour lies a paradox. On the one hand, it re-inforces the culture of teaching which stresses the *autonomy* of the teacher in the classroom, with great control over curriculum content, methods of teaching and learning, and pupil control. Leaving management to managers protects the autonomy of the teacher in the classroom. On the other hand, the culture is one of *dependence*, since it is the managers who make the key decisions affecting the school as a whole and the way it operates as a system. Because teachers are part of and are affected by the system as a whole, they depend on the nature and quality of the decisions made by 'the management'.

There is a further paradox. The most common and ubiquitous form of management is in fact *management of the classroom*, where both pupils and their teachers spend most of their time in school. Yet this is not usually seen as management. Indeed, the term management as used by teachers in their ordinary discourse has little to do with classroom life.

In consequence of all this, many teachers do not identify strongly with the school as a whole, the school as an institution. The focus of their work is the classroom within a culture of autonomy and dependence. Yet, as we have seen, development planning requires a holistic approach to the school, one which is undermined by the division between 'managers' and 'teachers'.

AN ALTERNATIVE CONCEPTION OF MANAGEMENT

We think it may be helpful in the context of development planning to shed some of these traditional and widespread understandings about the meaning of management.

Management is, as the textbooks tell us, about structures and procedures. However, because these have often evolved over time, they are taken for granted and regarded as fixed and immutable. We prefer the term *management arrangements*. This emphasizes that the content of management is a set of arrangements which are *chosen* by the members of an organization to help them to conduct their affairs and realize their aims. Because they are chosen, from a wide variety of possible arrangements, they can be changed or adapted according to circumstances and preferences.

The *content* of management is these arrangements which are chosen as the best or preferred mode of helping the school to undertake its work. But management is mainly about the people the arrangements are designed to serve.

Management is about people: management arrangements are what empower people. Empowerment, in short, is the *purpose* of management.

15

There is an endless possible variety of management arrangements. They vary according to the size, type and phase of the school as well as to the preferences of the governors, head and staff. We doubt whether there is an ideal set of arrangements, a recipe which all schools should follow. We do, however, think there are some *dimensions* shared by all management arrangements, whatever the particular set that is chosen by any individual school. These dimensions are the problems which all management arrangements have to solve if the people who work in and with the school are to be sufficiently empowered to achieve the school's aims through development planning.

There are three main dimensions common to all sets of management arrangements:

- The arrangements consist of *frameworks* which guide the actions of all who are involved in the school. Examples of frameworks are the school's aims and policies, and the systems for decision-making and consultation. Without clear frameworks, the school would soon lapse into confusion and conflict.

- The arrangements clarify *roles and responsibilities*. All who are involved in the school need to have a shared understanding of their respective roles and of *who* is taking responsibility for what. Well-designed frameworks are useless without clear roles and responsibilities.

- The arrangements promote ways in which the people involved can *work together* so that each person finds their particular role enjoyable and rewarding, and at the same time the aims of the school as a whole can be achieved successfully.

To devise management arrangements that solve the problems inherent in these three dimensions is a challenging task. Yet this challenge is already being attended to in many schools, since the pressures for change are creating a strain on the existing arrangements, and are leading governors, heads and staff to review traditional ways of managing the school. Governors in particular are looking for new ways of working with the head and staff which build upon the good relationships already established. Teachers are also realizing that the management of classrooms cannot be isolated from the management arrangements for the school as a whole. As budgets are delegated to schools, systems for managing finance and resources have to be created to complement or replace existing arrangements. The National Curriculum is leading to a new approach to the whole curriculum, to the deployment of teachers and to the organization of teaching, learning and assessment.

Such changes are leading everyone in schools to rethink the nature of management: what it is and what it needs to become. Management as empowerment may require a transformation of the school's culture.

DEVELOPMENT PLANNING AND THE CULTURE OF THE SCHOOL

Successful schools realize that development planning is about creating a school culture which will support the planning and management of changes of many different kinds.

School culture is difficult to define, but is best thought of as the procedures, values and expectations that guide people's behaviour within an organization. The school's culture is essentially 'the way we do things around here'.

The management arrangements are the most vital expression of the school's culture. Creating a particular school culture requires management arrangements of a certain character. An important aspect of the character of effective schools is that management is not the unique task of those at the apex of a hierarchy but a shared responsibility of all who are involved in the school. A culture which proclaims that heads (and deputies) manage but teachers teach is not conducive to effective development planning, which requires a culture in which everyone is a manager of some kind. Of course, heads and deputies have specific management functions; but teachers and others also have management functions. All contribute to the culture of the school, so all should contribute to the management arrangements the purpose of which is to empower. It is this shared approach to management of all that happens in the school which allows the management of change to be successful.

This cannot be achieved if the prevailing school culture is one where 'managers' are designing changes whilst teachers desperately cling to practices they have come to trust and are excluded from management, or one where teachers strive for change but the 'managers' resist adjustments to how the school is managed. Nor can it be achieved when management has only a marginal relationship to teaching and learning in classrooms. The ultimate goal of development and change is an improvement of the quality of teaching and learning in the classroom. The focus and test of development is what happens in classrooms. The contribution of classroom teachers to the management arrangements is therefore crucial.

DEVELOPMENT AND MAINTENANCE

Changing a school's culture and approach to management can begin only from where a school now is. At present, schools are facing two kinds of pressure. The first is that of *development*. Schools cannot remain as they now are if they are to implement recent reforms. The second pressure is that of *maintenance*. Schools need to maintain some continuity with their present and past practices, partly to provide the stability which is the foundation of new developments and partly because the reforms do not by any means change everything that schools now do. There is thus a tension between development and maintenance. The management arrangements have to sustain both (see Figure 3.1): the way this is achieved is an expression of the school's culture.

All schools are having to plan in more sophisticated ways than in the past. In the light of the National Curriculum requirements, the curriculum requires more careful and elaborate planning. This has consequences for the planning of staff, and for their professional development and INSET. In many schools this has to be underpinned by better financial planning, especially where the school takes more responsibility for buildings and premises. All this may require changes in the management arrangements. On the one hand, these arrangements must support maintenance – the preservation of what has worked well to give the school its stability and its reputation. On the other hand, they must also provide a means of dealing effectively with new developments.

Development planning is therefore about *both* ensuring maintenance *and* supporting development. Development planning is not likely to be successful if the existing management arrangements are assumed to be adequate for supporting development simply because they have worked well in the past in ensuring maintenance. More than a minor adjustment to the management arrangements is likely to be needed.

There are no arrows in Figure 3.1 to link together its five features. Its purpose is not to describe the relationships or to explain them. It is a *heuristic* diagram. Each school needs to work out how the elements are currently related to one another, and how they ought to be related to promote development planning and school improvement.

To this end it might be useful to ask questions such as:

- How do existing plans and planning activities (e.g. for the curriculum or staffing or finance/resources) support development as well as maintenance?

- Does our approach to development planning support maintenance as well as development?

- Does development planning challenge some current aspects of maintenance?

- How is it possible for today's new development to become part of tomorrow's maintenance?

The last question is perhaps the most important. An aim of the development plan is to move a new development into the school's maintenance activities. This is what is meant by consolidating a change. The key to this transition is the quality of the management arrangements.

When the pace of change is great, there is a tendency for teachers to feel overwhelmed by new developments. This can easily lead to overload and to such a dilution of effort that little gets done properly because it is inadequately managed.

To avoid innovation overload, the school should be firm in its resolve to prioritize, and should not attempt to develop everything at once. It should seek to accomplish a few developmental priorities as best it can and continue to engage in its maintenance activities as well as it would have done in any case. Development planning controls the range of developments undertaken in any one year, but leads to the adjustment of the management arrangements so that innovations can succeed and be consolidated within maintenance. This is the process of change.

It is apparent from the project's research that from the moment when the school decides to embark on development planning, governors, head and staff need to:

- accept that the process of development planning is as important as the careful construction of the plan as a document: successful implementation depends on the character and quality of the *process* of planning as well as on the specific content of the plan;

- remember that the process may well involve *cultural change*;

- find ways in which *every* teacher, in the 'new' culture, becomes a

Figure 3.1 *The management of planning*

manager of change, with particular roles and responsibilities but also with a grasp of, and commitment to, the process as a whole;

- review and *continually adjust* the management arrangements to empower all who are engaged in the planning and implementation of change.

THE HEAD AND THE MANAGEMENT ARRANGEMENTS

The quality of the head's leadership is the single most important factor in the success of a school. The head also plays the most important role in the determination of the management arrangements. They are likely to be effective when the head:

- *inspires* commitment to the school's mission which gives direction and purpose to its work;

- *co-ordinates the work of the school* by allocating roles and delegating responsibilities within structures that support collaboration between the school and its partners;

- is actively and visibly *involved* in the planning and implementation of change, but is ready to delegate and value the contribution of colleagues;

- knows how to *listen and respond* positively to the ideas and complaints of colleagues, governors and parents without feeling threatened;

- is a *skilled communicator*, keeping everyone informed about important decisions and events;

- has the capacity to *stand back* from daily life in order to challenge what is taken for granted, to anticipate problems and to spot opportunities;

- *cares* passionately for the school, its members and reputation, but has the ability objectively to appraise strengths and weaknesses in order to preserve and build upon the best of current practice and to remedy deficiencies;

- emphasizes the *quality of teaching and learning* about which he or she has high expectations of all staff and all pupils, whilst recognizing that support and encouragement are needed for everyone to give of their best;

- is *enthusiastic about innovation*, but judicious in controlling the pace of change;

- *keeps paperwork to a minimum*, since it takes too much time to write long papers, which few people will read anyway.

Where the deputies and senior staff share these qualities, an appropriate set of management arrangements is most likely to be chosen.

It is important that the head and senior staff take the lead in helping everyone to develop an agreed perspective on how the tension between development and maintenance might be resolved. This is not easily done, often because there is already a poor balance between maintenance and development in the work of 'senior management'. Many senior staff, and especially deputies, have a reduced teaching load because they spend so much time on management. Of what do these 'management' activities consist? Research has shown that most of these are brief, ad hoc responses to relatively minor matters, such as:

- checking that each class has a teacher;

- dealing with pupils referred to them;

- answering telephone calls;

- meeting visitors;

- resolving small problems raised by staff;

- maintaining the flow of paperwork and routine administration.

In short, senior staff shore up short-term *maintenance* and, for a surprisingly large proportion of the time, exercise few of the high-level skills appropriate to their age, status, experience and pay. But that such work needs to be done by someone is undeniable.

The striking feature of the daily lives of senior staff is how little time they have to devote in a sustained way to *development*. They are often so overwhelmed by maintenance that development issues tend to be dealt with in the early morning, in the evening or at weekends. We have found, not surprisingly, that the draft of the development plan is sometimes written by the senior management team and then presented to both governors and staff, with relatively little consultation or involvement. The inevitable result is that the teachers and others, on whom the burden of implementation falls, have little 'ownership' of the plan.

It is one of the tasks of the head and the senior staff to devise management arrangements whereby:

- they, the staff and all who are to be involved in the development plan have opportunities to give sustained attention to the nature of development planning and to the construction of the plan itself;

- the slogan 'every teacher is a manager' becomes a reality through a more equitable distribution of both development and maintenance activities;

- senior staff make the empowerment of others, rather than routine maintenance, the central purpose of their work.

To put it another way, many schools may find their present conception of management is as portrayed in Figure 3.2, which is another heuristic diagram where each school can draw its own arrows to express the direction and strength of the relations

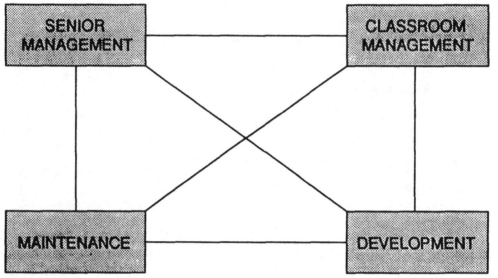

Figure 3.2 *Tensions in management*

between the components. The very different conception of management as empowerment required in development planning is suggested in Figure 3.3..

REVIEWING THE MANAGEMENT ARRANGEMENTS

Whilst the head undoubtedly plays the major role, management and the arrangements to support it are a collective activity and responsibility. It falls to the head, however, to take the lead in reviewing the school's management arrangements to support development planning, since it is the head's commitment to management as empowerment which must underpin the transformation of the management arrangements.

One way to approach such a review is by considering in detail the three dimensions of the management arrangements and then judging the extent to which the existing arrangements meet the demands of development planning.

The following definitions of the three dimensions of the management arrangements are not descriptions of the *form* the arrangements should take. That is a matter for the choice of each school. Rather the lists under each dimension are some of the tasks to which a school should pay attention in making its choice of arrangements. The dimensions are common to all schools, large and small, primary, middle, secondary and special. The actual arrangements chosen to allow the tasks for each dimension to be accomplished will, however, be unique to the school. We have drawn the details of the three dimensions from schools where development planning is most successful. They may be used as a guide for a school to review the character and quality of its management arrangements.

Some elements in each dimension are discussed more fully in Part 5 of this book, and could be used as a resource for activities on a professional training day or at meetings.

ESTABLISHING FRAMEWORKS

Frameworks – policies, systems, and strategies – provide the structures within which action for change takes place. They are the guides to action, the scaffolding that supports the educational work of the school, both maintenance and development. Clear frameworks give direction and purpose to development planning and support its management.

Establishing frameworks for governors, heads and staff means:

- turning aims and goals into brief, *written policy statements* that provide consistency in interpretation and unambiguous guides to action (Resource File 1);

- devising *strategies* for change and for the further development of existing policies, within which tactics may be chosen (Resource File 2);

- making *meetings* effective by deciding on their purpose, functions, terms of reference and cycles (Resource File 3);

- keeping permanent committees to a minimum and creating *task groups* with a short, fixed lease of life;

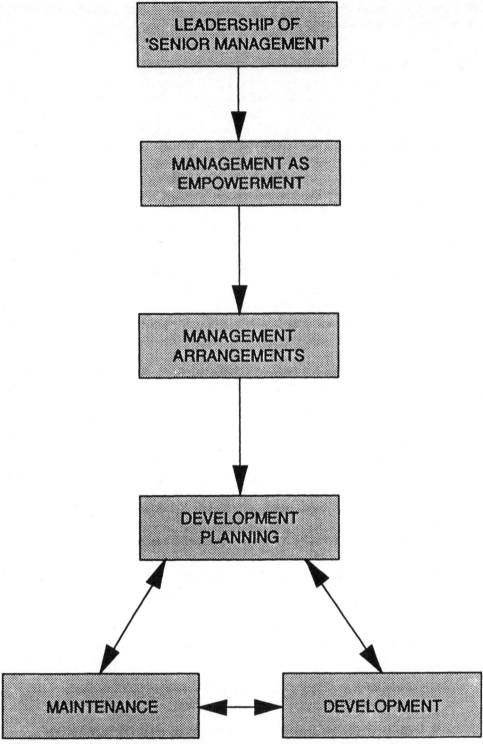

Figure 3.3 *Management as empowerment*

- being more effective in the *management of time*: to make room for new commitments, some existing activities may need to cease;

- deciding who needs to know about what and when, with appropriate channels of *communication and reporting*, especially on the progress of the plan;

- devising a means of judging the *extent and quality of progress* in developmental work;

- integrating the school's system for *monitoring and evaluating* its activities with the LEA's approach to monitoring and evaluation (Resource File 4);

- co-ordinating *planning cycles* within the school and between the school and the LEA (Resource File 5).

CLARIFYING ROLES

Frameworks serve as the backcloth for action. To build the confidence and security of those involved with development planning, roles and responsibilities for both development and maintenance need to be clarified.

Clarifying roles for governors, heads and staff means:

- working out *new relationships* between governors, head and staff (Resource File 6);

- providing a *flexible range of roles* and responsibilities to involve everyone in the management and development of the school as a whole;

- recognizing that *management development* should support the head and senior staff and help in preparing others for such roles, but should also help *all staff* to share effectively in the management of the school;

- recognizing that *'horizontal' teams* (across subjects, departments and year groups) are potentially more creative than 'vertical' (or hierarchical) management.

WORKING TOGETHER

The successful implementation of strategies depends on the quality of relationships among those involved with the plan. Effective planning requires collaboration and co-ordination between the school and its partners.

Working together for governors, heads and staff means:

- recognizing the advantages of *collaboration and teamwork* both within the school and with the school's partners (Resource File 7);

- promoting *new forms of collaboration* between teachers, and between the school and its partners, to support both the work of the school as a whole and the work of individual teachers in classrooms;

- *expecting all to contribute* to the school's development and valuing the distinctive contributions made by governors, head and staff;

- giving everyone *opportunities to display leadership*, since the capacity for leadership does not depend on age, status or position in a hierarchy;

- devising a *staff development policy* that links individual professional development to institutional development (Resource File 8);

- establishing a *partnership* with LEA officers.

Through a review and revision of its management arrangements a school begins to transform its culture to support effective development planning. At the same time, the process of development planning will itself generate changes to the management arrangements and to the culture of the school. It is a matter of fine judgement to decide which aspects of the management arrangements need to be changed before beginning work on development planning. But it is unwise to delay just because conditions in the school do not seem wholly conducive; they rarely are. The work of development planning will itself help to promote better conditions.

And it is important to remember that changes to the management arrangements can be selected as a priority in the plan. That few schools usually do so reflects the fact that they have not thought this relevant to the plan rather than because it is not appropriate as part of the plan.

Problems will be overcome as the people involved gain confidence and skill in the process. Recognizing that the appropriate management arrangements will evolve progressively to support new roles and relationships is itself a step in changing the culture of the school.

The theme of this chapter has been management as empowerment. The ideas we have offered are not prescriptions to be followed or models to be imitated. It is a chapter of questions which we believe to be worth asking in any school, rather than answers derived from our work on the project. Learning to ask the right questions of itself is more empowering of a school than being given other people's second-hand answers.

When everyone

- is open about the planning and management of change,

- gives development planning the time and status it needs,

- draws upon the experience, talents and suggestions of others,

- is willing to learn by making some mistakes,

there arises a climate of partnership focused on enhancing the quality of teaching and learning in the school. This is the heart of development planning.

PART TWO

PROCESS

Development planning is a whole-school process. The account of the process in this part is applicable to most schools – the majority of primary schools and smaller middle, secondary and special schools. In very small primary schools, the process is simpler in some regards (there are too few staff to create elaborate teams) and more difficult in others (there are not enough staff to carry forward an ambitious plan). In larger middle and secondary schools, the process can be applied both to the school as a whole and to subject departments or faculties. They may well conduct an individual audit and then construct, implement and evaluate a departmental or faculty development plan. We advise, however, that the development plan of even a very large school should be more than a collection of department/faculty plans: there should always be some priorities which transcend the department or faculty and develop the school or college as a whole.

Chapter 4

Getting Started

In schools where the idea of a development plan is novel, some careful attention should be given to getting started. Staff and governors need the confidence and commitment to believe that a development plan is indeed a helpful way forward. *It is dangerous to rush into development planning*: if it is done badly, it will demoralize teachers and weaken further attempts to improve forward planning and the management of change. Before embarking on development planning, a school should ascertain the LEA's policy, and its provision of support and INSET. It may be helpful in preparing the ground for governors and staff to consider the value of development planning by asking the following questions:

- How will it help improve the quality of the education we provide?

- How will it help us to manage change and cope with 'innovation overload'?

- How will it help us enhance the partnership between teachers, governors, parents and the LEA?

- How will it help the staff to work together in realizing the aims of the school?

Questions such as these might be addressed in one or more of the following activities:

- The head and governors discuss the advantages of development planning, or a committee of the governors and staff consider this book and advise the governing body how it might benefit the school.

- Discussing development planning with LEA officers.

- Devoting a staff meeting or training day to this book.

- Arranging a visit by the head, some governors and staff to a school which has successful experience with development planning, or inviting people from such a school to talk about their experience.

- Staff of two or three small schools meet together to discuss this book.

Schools often find such awareness-raising activities helpful as an introduction to development planning.

Despite such awareness-raising activities some schools may still feel that they are 'unready' to embark on development planning. The criterion of 'readiness' is a double-edged sword. If a school waits for ideal conditions then it may never begin development planning; if it tries too much too soon then failure may result. As we made clear in Chapter 3, our view is that it is unwise to delay even if conditions are not ideal: rather, it is better to embark on development planning judiciously. Paradoxically, more is learnt from doing than planning.

We have discussed two strategies for getting started:

- *awareness-raising* (in this chapter);
- *reviewing the school's management arrangements* (in Chapter 3).

Both of these activities may suggest issues for possible priorities in the development plan.

There are a number of other guidelines that are useful when beginning development planning:

- Do not be too ambitious, build on early success: start small, think big.
- Build an understanding of the process of development planning.
- Generate ownership and commitment by involving as many of the school's partners as feasible by providing early training and devolving responsibility.
- Focus on priorities that are fundamental to the school, such as generating collaboration, as well as those that are important and specific, such as aspects of the National Curriculum.

It is in these ways that a school prepares itself for the process of development planning.

Chapter 5

Carrying out a School Audit

Planning needs to start from where the school now is. A development plan is about the management of change and development. Properly understood, *change* is just another word for *growth*. To assist the process of growth, one needs to know where one is *growing from* as much as where one is *growing towards*.

An audit involves questioning current provision and practice in a systematic and self-critical way: comparing what the school is striving to achieve with what is actually happening. The audit clarifies the nature of a school's weaknesses and guides the action needed to put things right.

The *purposes* of the audit are:

- to clarify the state of the school, and to identify strengths on which to build and weaknesses to be rectified;

- to provide a basis for selecting priorities for development.

A strategic approach to the audit involves:

- taking account of the context;

- deciding upon the content;

- deciding on strategies;

- clarifying roles;

- using the outcomes of specific audits.

THE CONTEXT FOR THE AUDIT

A school should set its audit within the context of:

- the school's mission;

- the aims and values of the school;

- policies and initiatives of central government and the LEA;

- recent reviews of the school;

- targets set at teacher appraisal interviews;

- other views and perspectives.

Mission is a powerful motivating force for school improvement. It is composed of the shared images and values of governors, staff, pupils and parents. Building the mission and generating ownership towards it is a key task. What is the school's mission? Does everyone share in the mission? Are the policies and priorities consistent with the mission?

Aims of the school reflect its mission. As they describe the fundamental purpose of the school, so they are important criteria by which the school judges itself. Which aims are being most fully achieved in practice, and why? Which aims are least well achieved, and what might be done to obtain full achievement?

Policies and initiatives from central government and the LEA influence the aims of the school and provide some of the grounds for selecting priorities during the construction phase. Can the initiatives be grafted onto past achievements? Do they help to remedy known deficiencies?

Recent reviews of the school, either in the form of a school self-evaluation or an inspection/review by the LEA or HMI, will make the audit simpler. Was the outcome of the review accepted by the governors and staff? What action was taken in the light of the review? How might LEA officers help in the audit process?

Targets set at teacher appraisal interviews represent individual teachers' views of their own professional development priorities, as compared with the school's development plan priorities. When taken together the teachers' appraisal targets provide an important agenda for action for the school as a whole. How might appraisal targets support development plan priorities, and vice versa? How can the process of appraisal be integrated with development planning and the school's management arrangements?

Views and perspectives of individuals and groups reveal how the school is seen by staff, governors, parents, pupils and the community. How can existing consultative processes contribute to the audit? What new ones might be needed?

Carrying out an audit involves clarifying the roles of governors, head and staff in order to answer three questions:

- Who decides the areas for specific audit?

- Who carries out each specific audit?

- Who draws together the various elements of the audit in a summary overview?

Although these roles will vary according to the size and phase of school, there are some common patterns. Selecting the areas for specific audit will usually be done by the head, following discussions with governors and staff. The responsibility for carrying out the audit normally rests with one teacher or a team. The head or a senior member of staff summarizes the result of the audit.

THE CONTENT OF THE AUDIT

Carrying out a *full* audit of all provision and practice is very time-consuming. In the past, schemes of school-based review demanded a thorough examination of the life and work of the school, and two or three terms were often set aside for this. Development work for subsequent years was then planned on the basis of this review. Today the pressure for change makes this approach less appropriate. It is now advisable to carry out a series of small-scale focused or *specific audits* in key areas and in implementing the action plans that may result from these enquiries. A planned series of specific audits creates a *rolling programme* which provides a picture of the school built up over successive years.

The school might select any of the following areas for specific audit in a single year:

- pupils' diversity and achievements;
- curriculum provision and access;
- assessment and recording;
- pupil attendance, punctuality and behaviour;
- teaching styles and methods;
- responsibilities of the teaching staff;
- school management and organization;
- relationships with parents;
- partnership with the local community;
- links with other schools and colleges;
- school, LEA and national documents;
- resources.

Two of these, curriculum provision and resources, require an annual audit, so more detailed guidance on them is provided.

Auditing the Curriculum

Schools are reviewing their curriculum as a whole to meet the requirements of the National Curriculum. Schools therefore need to:

- check whether the planned curriculum meets the statutory requirements;
- identify possible gaps or overlap between subject areas;
- ensure that where two or more subjects or activities are concerned with the same range of objectives, this is recognized and used positively;
- plan the provision of cross-curricular themes, dimensions and skills;
- analyse the curriculum for each year-group in terms of curricular objectives within and outside the National Curriculum;

- decide in which parts of the school curriculum to locate work leading to the National Curriculum and other school curricular objectives;

- assess how much teaching time is available and how best to use it;

- compare *planned* provision with *actual* provision;

- judge whether curriculum issues need to be among the priorities for development.

Auditing the Resources

The governors and head need to ensure an appropriate match between plans for development and the use of resources. A development plan needs to be supported by financial and resource planning.

Account needs to be taken of:

- how and why the school used its resources during the previous year;

- how the school judges and ensures effective and efficient use of resources;

- how development planning should fashion the use of resources rather than being fashioned by them at a late stage.

Effective auditing of resources will make construction of the plan easier and more realistic. During the audit a person or group should make use of existing information, or gather information, about the deployment of resources between years and budget headings. This involves considering:

- the use made of the expertise and time of teachers and support staff;

- expenditure on materials, consumables and equipment;

- running costs such as heating, lighting and telephone bills;

- the use of resources from outside the school's immediate budget, e.g. TVEI, GEST;

- resources or income the school has generated (and may be able to generate) for itself;

- the use of accommodation.

DECIDING ON STRATEGIES

Once certain aspects of the school have been selected for specific audit, those given responsibility for each area choose strategies. There are three main strategies from which to select:

- getting an external perspective;

- using a published scheme;

- designing your own approach.

The focus and scale of any audit should be manageable within available resources, especially time. Some of the strengths and limitations of different strategies are listed below.

Getting an External Perspective

Different perspectives on the school are provided by parents, LEA officers, HMIs, consultants from higher education and 'critical friends'. These views aid the governors, head and staff in developing an overall picture of their school. Most useful are the external perspectives that build up a picture of the school over time and provide benchmarks for gauging school development – LEA inspections and, in secondary schools, TVEI reviews. See Box 5.1 for the strengths and limitations of the 'external perspective' strategy.

Box 5.1 *The 'external perspective' strategy: strengths and limitations*

Strengths	Limitations
• provides a dispassionate view, and a chance for staff to talk through problems with outsiders	• timing of visit/inspection may be inappropriate for school needs or planning cycle
• limited time-scale reduces demands on staff	• might not focus on school's concerns and may result in breadth rather than depth
• tells schools what they are doing well besides highlighting weaknesses	• external perspectives on their own do not necessarily lead to development
• provides the possibility of bringing new ideas into the school and encourages staff to question what they take for granted	• may neglect the existing inner strengths of the school

Using a Published Scheme

A range of schemes and advice are available on planning school review and development. The GRIDS (Guidelines for Review and Internal Development in Schools) handbooks, now distributed by the National Curriculum Council (NCC), are an example of a published scheme that has been widely used. Some schools find it easier to start with a published scheme but move on to modify it or devise their own in later cycles. The GRIDS approach, in particular, is amenable to adaptation: its major advantage is that it can accommodate a variety of audit strategies. The NCC's Curriculum Guidance No. 3, *The Whole Curriculum*, is another example of a published scheme: it contains advice on conducting curriculum audits. Box 5.2 shows the strengths and limitations of the 'published scheme' strategy.

Designing Your Own Approach

School-generated approaches to audit use various techniques adapted to the individual school's situation. These can include: discussions and debate during meetings, conferences and training days; professional development discussions and teacher appraisal interviews; questionnaires; scrutinizing documents such as teaching materials and school policies; systematic observation; and analysing statistical records. Pupils can also be involved in a number of ways – discussions with teachers, surveys of their views or the recommendations of the school council. The strengths and limitations of the 'own approach' strategy can be seen in Box 5.3. The choice of strategy will depend on its appropriateness to the area selected for specific audit.

Although the strategies have been treated separately in this section, schools often use them in combination:

- In one school, the external perspective offered by an LEA officer and external consultant provided the impetus for the school to explore particular issues in further depth by choosing their own approach.

- In another school, following a GRIDS review, some staff decided to write a personal account to a specific issue. The teachers' individual accounts not only illuminated the issues but also made suggestions which were subsequently incorporated into action plans.

- One school integrated the outcomes of staff appraisal (the identification of staff strengths and professional development needs) with the outcomes of the audit (the identification of school strengths and areas for development). Links between individual development and institutional development were then made through the personal action plans resulting from the appraisal. The head, following a series of appraisal interviews, became convinced that new science guidelines needed developing. The production of these guidelines subsequently became the focus of action plans that incorporated teachers' appraisal targets and a staff development programme.

- Some appraisal schemes specifically link whole-school review to teacher appraisal. In one LEA, for example, a GRIDS review precedes by a term the introduction of teacher appraisal. The areas of development identified by the review provide part of the agenda for the appraisal interview. As a result many teachers see appraisal and whole-school development as a more purposeful and integrated process.

Box 5.2 *The 'published scheme' strategy: strengths and limitations*

Strengths	Limitations
• every staff member's view is usually canvassed	• not specific to the school and often neglects the individual context
• designed to be comprehensive in scope	• implicit values of the schemes are not always apparent
• is less time-consuming than devising one's own approach	• staff often perceive the use of a questionnaire as being too mechanical
• seen to be objective and impartial	• may not be appropriate for use in obtaining views of the school's partners

Box 5.3 *The 'own approach' strategy: strengths and limitations*

Strengths	Limitations
• generates 'ownership' and commitment to the findings, and encourages staff to consider the whole-school perspective	• may take considerable staff time and resources in preparation, administration and follow-up
• focuses on issues of particular importance to the school	• key questions may not be asked because those in the school did not perceive them as important
• can be easily adapted to consider the concerns of particular groups	• staff may lack the skills required for an in-depth audit
• can be planned to fit into the normal work of the school	• the validity of the approach may be questioned by some

CLARIFYING ROLES

The audit is easier if it is carefully planned and responsibility for particular aspects is shared out. For example:

- *A curriculum leader* in primary school leads a small group to scrutinize a selection of pupil work from different year-groups to examine progression and continuity and their relation to the National Curriculum;

- *A department* in a secondary school reviews its curriculum provision; assesses the implications of the National Curriculum for that subject; analyses policies and practice on pupil assessment; analyses examination/test results; reviews pupils' written work to check on progression and continuity.

- *A team* considers relations with parents and the wider community.

- *The head, a deputy or a senior teacher* leads a working party on topics such as cross-curricular issues, curriculum provision as a whole, pupil attendance, the school's documentation.

- *The staff development or INSET co-ordinator* leads a working party to review staff development, INSET provision and dissemination, teacher appraisal, care of probationer teachers.

Lead persons for each aspect of the audit need a clear brief, with a time-scale, and should produce a short summary of the main findings and areas for development.

USING THE OUTCOMES OF SPECIFIC AUDITS

Most schools find five outcomes to a specific audit:

- *The audit reveals strengths*. Schools do not always know their strengths. In one secondary school, some staff identified 'improving links with the primary school' as a key priority. It turned out that they were unaware of the extent of existing links developed by colleagues. Improved communication about existing practice was what was required. A school may also choose to audit a perceived strength in order to learn more systematically from its own practice.

- *Some weaknesses can be remedied easily*. Some problems which are identified during audit can be solved quickly and easily without an action plan.

- *A specific audit becomes a priority*. If an unusually detailed audit is felt to be necessary in a particular area, it is better to make this a priority within the development plan and draw up an action plan accordingly. Development in this area then becomes possible in subsequent cycles.

- *The audit provides the basis for action planning*. Where the report on the audit identifies in detail the work to be done, this provides the basis for action plans at a later stage.

- *A list of potential priorities is identified*. To help with the final selection of priorities, a report on the audit is prepared which identifies potential priorities together with a rough estimate of the work needing to be done.

In this way, the audit paves the way for the identification of priorities for development.

CHECKLIST OF QUESTIONS

- Has the audit taken account of all the appropriate contexts?

- Is it appropriate to do a full-scale audit or focus on specific areas over several years?

- Has the school chosen the most appropriate strategy or strategies for carrying out the audit?

- Is there an audit of the curriculum and of resources?

- Have roles and responsibilities and time-scales for the audit been clearly defined?

- How will the outcomes of the audit help the choice of priorities?

- Will the audit result in a short summary document of findings and recommendations to provide a basis for constructing the development plan?

Chapter 6

Drawing up the Development Plan

The more carefully the development plan is constructed, the easier it will be to manage the process of implementation.

Plans are constructed in *detail* for the year ahead. The longer-term priorities for the following two or three years are described in *outline*. This gives continuity and coherence to the school's development, whilst leaving room in the plan to meet future demands arising from national or local initiatives and the school's changing needs.

The main task of the construction process is to decide which issues should be priorities for the first year of the plan, and which must be postponed to the second, third or even later years.

The plan should be realistic, neither too ambitious nor insufficiently demanding. We suggest that there should be no more than three or four major priorities, though each priority may contain a number of elements. If the plan is realistic, it is much more likely to be implemented.

Plan construction involves:

- taking account of the context;

- consulting about possible priorities;

- making a decision on the priorities;

- writing up and publicizing the plan.

TAKING ACCOUNT OF THE CONTEXT

The governors, head and staff should consider all the factors affecting planning, which arise from six main sources (see Figure 6.1):

- the mission and aims of the school;

- national policies and initiatives, e.g. the National Curriculum and assessment, staff appraisal, TVEI;

- LEA policies and initiatives, e.g. records of achievement, school–industry links;

- school initiatives, e.g. targets from teacher appraisal;

- issues emerging from the audit;

- finance available.

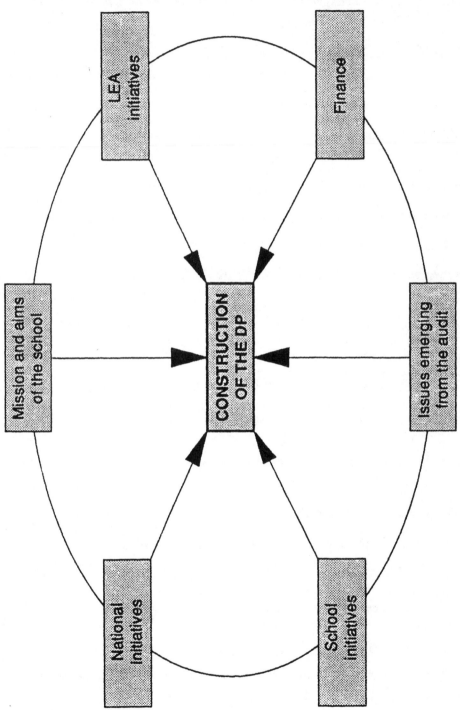

Figure 6.1 *The context of the development plan*

The selected priorities reflect the school's response to and synthesis of national and local policies and initiatives. The plan must acquire its own coherence and relate closely to the aims and values of the school.

CONSULTING ABOUT POSSIBLE PRIORITIES

The plan is most likely to be sound if, from the start, everyone understands that they can contribute to its construction as well as to its implementation.

In most schools there will be no shortage of ideas about how the school might develop. The more widely the school consults, the greater the number of possible priorities that will be suggested. There is likely to be a diversity of views among staff and governors. Parents and pupils usually contribute fresh, positive ideas. The support staff, the parent–teacher association and the school council should all be consulted. LEA officers are also an important source of advice.

In some schools new procedures and techniques for consultation may be needed. Consultation needs to be seen by all involved as a worthwhile process in which views are taken seriously.

MAKING A DECISION ON THE PRIORITIES

Consultation will lead to a 'long-list' of priorities. The critical stage of plan construction has now been reached: a small number of priorities has to be selected for the first year of the plan, and others deferred to the second, third and later years.

A rag-bag of priorities does not make a good plan. A collection of priorities put together on an arbitrary or ad hoc basis creates problems in implementation and makes it difficult to justify the selection.

The choice of priorities is guided by two principles. The plan must be:

- *manageable*: the risk of trying to do too much too quickly must be avoided;

- *coherent*: the priorities must be placed in a sequence that makes implementation easier.

Manageability and coherence require careful thought about the number of chosen priorities and the relationships between them, both within any one year and between years. Major priorities, such as those deriving from the National Curriculum and new forms of assessment, are best divided into a series of annual 'chunks' over a longer period. This makes even very ambitious developments more coherent and more manageable.

It is obviously highly desirable that there should be a high level of agreement about the plan among governors, head and staff – as well as with the school's partners. When the plan has been designed to be manageable and coherent, a clear and explicit rationale can be provided for it. This helps people to reach agreement on the plan and to explain why some of the possible priorities cannot be included in the short term.

Plan construction is easier when governors, head and staff:

- consider urgency, need and desirability;

- estimate size and scope;

- distinguish between root and branch innovations;

- forge links between priorities.

Consider Urgency, Need and Desirability

Some priorities are chosen on the grounds that they are urgent or unavoidable; the legal requirements of the National Curriculum fall into this category. Other possible priorities will be proposed because they are needed to improve the school. Some may be urgent, whilst others may be desirable but less pressing.

Estimate Size and Scope

Larger priorities which extend over two or more years, such as National Curriculum or cross-curricular provision, need very careful planning and management. Others can be implemented during a single year.

Estimating size and scope is easier if preliminary estimates about the projected time-scale for a priority, the amount of work required (including resources) and the number of people who might be involved have been made. Making such a judgement is important if the school is to make a sensible decision about how many priorities to select for any one year.

The greatest danger is taking on too many priorities of considerable scope and complexity in a single year, rendering the plan unmanageable in practice.

Schools should undertake a very small number of *major* priorities of considerable size and scope in a single year. Once a decision on these has been made, the school can then add the number of small or minor priorities that can also be successfully implemented, in the light of the capacity of the staff and any of the school's partners who may be involved.

Distinguish between Root and Branch Innovations

It was pointed out earlier that change is just another word for growth.

In terms of this metaphor, a school may lack roots of sufficient strength and depth to support the branches of innovation which represent its growth from existing practice. Development planning involves two kinds of change: *root innovations* that generate the base on which other, or *branch innovations*, can be sustained. Strong roots to support many aspects of the development plan are provided by, for example, good management arrangements, a well-designed staff development policy, or a history of collaborative work among the staff and with the school's partners. When such roots are lacking, there is a danger that some of the planned branch innovations will wither and die.

Two questions can usefully be asked about any possible priority:

- Can it be treated as a branch innovation with good prospects for successful implementation because the school has already established relevant roots to support it?

43

- When it is implemented, will it serve as a root for future branch innovations to be implemented in later years of the plan?

Thus, if the school is considering whether to introduce a whole-school policy on assessment, marking and recording, the existence of such a policy in parts of the school (e.g. for language and mathematics) will act as relevant roots to make implementation easier. The whole-school policy on assessment, once implemented, will become the root to support changes required for assessing, recording and reporting on achievement in the National Curriculum. If no roots exist for a possible priority, then the school may decide that the necessary root innovations should take precedence in the development plan.

In these ways, the distinction between 'root' and 'branch' helps in deciding upon the sequence of priorities. Because the management arrangements serve as a root to so many innovations, adjustments to them will be a strong candidate for an early priority in many schools.

Forge Links between Priorities

Schools frequently choose a relatively diverse set of priorities in any one year. The main advantages are that developments are spread across a wide range of the school's work and it is easier to involve the whole staff and a variety of partners in the action plans. Yet it is also possible to choose some priorities which are closely related to one another. This fosters collaboration between staff and partners working on different targets and leads to greater progress. A secondary school, for example, might look for a common priority – such as new teaching styles or links with industry and business – which cuts across different initiatives, such as TVEI, Records of Achievement, and the National Curriculum.

The task of deciding the priorities is best undertaken by a team, such as a group of staff chaired by the head or a joint working party of staff and governors. The team constructs a draft development plan about which all the governors and all the staff should be consulted. The head plays a key role in seeking as much consensus as possible about the draft plan, which is then presented formally to the governors for their consideration and approval.

The pace of the plan construction process will vary from school to school. In general terms, the larger the size of school the more formal the process of consultation. In some smaller primary schools, however, the long list of priorities may be so obvious that the head, staff and governors can move rapidly towards agreeing a draft plan.

TWO ILLUSTRATIONS OF PLAN CONSTRUCTION

Choosing Priorities

Figure 6.2 illustrates how a chart summarizing the four issues affecting the choice from possible priorities can help decision-making. This primary school already has some experience of development planning. Language had been a priority in earlier years, so the guidelines developed then serve as a root to support the branch inno-

POSSIBLE PRIORITIES

ISSUES AFFECTING CHOICE	Language	Assessment and record keeping	Home/school partnership	Staff appraisal	School environment and playground
Unavoidable	National Curriculum requirements for English	National requirement			
Urgent			Parent concern over National Curriculum to be addressed		
Desirable				Should help professional development	Pupils see as highly desirable
Large size and scope (resources)		Audit suggests much work needed			Potentially expensive and slow
Small size and scope (resources)	Language policy and practice developed over two previous years		Improving home newsletter and meetings for parents	Staff identified this in the audit and are keen to make it work	
Strong roots	Guidelines on language already exist			Recent improvement to staff development policy	Some work done already
Weak roots		Good collaboration between staff will support the work	Parental attendance at meetings is variable		
Strong links to other priorities	Important to develop link with assessment priority	Link to language in first instance	Use to help parental involvement in language	Will support first two priorities	
Weak links to other priorities					Indirect – via improved morale

Figure 6.2 *Choosing priorities*

vation of the National Curriculum requirements in English and the involvement of parents in reading. Assessment and recording is not, in the view of staff and LEA officers, as good as it might be and further work is now required in this area. Improved collaboration among staff resulting from work on the language policy will serve as a root. A better assessment policy will enhance the continuing work on language.

Appraisal had been put on one side, but governors and staff believe this will now help to take forward the school's evolving policy and practice for professional development. This will then act as a root to many future innovations.

Improving the environment has been of long-standing concern, and the entrance hall and display areas have been improved recently. The costs of improving the playground are considerable and it is unlikely that major work can be undertaken this year.

A chart, as exemplified in Figure 6.2, can help in making a decision about the final choice of priorities. It also helps in explaining to everyone the reasons behind the choice. Those whose preferred priorities cannot be fitted into the plan at this point can see why other priorities are being chosen.

Sequencing Priorities

The sequencing of priorities *between years* is much easier once a school learns to use early priorities as roots for branch innovations in subsequent years. Figure 6.3 illustrates the first development plan of a secondary school.

Two priorities are concerned with the curriculum. The first is a continuing priority of implementing the National Curriculum over successive years in accordance with the national timetable, beginning with the core subjects. It has been agreed that each subject department should construct its own action plans for the National Curriculum, with a deputy head co-ordinating work between departments. The second consists of cross-curricular provision, beginning with a working party to formulate a policy (aided by the NCC's Curriculum Guidance No. 3, *The Whole Curriculum*) and to propose changes to the school's management arrangements to support cross-departmental co-ordination. The sequence of work on cross-curricular themes has been influenced by the fact that the school's best current practice is in health education and careers education, and improvements here will serve as roots for subsequent work on citizenship, environmental education and economic and industrial understanding. Changes to the PSE programme (including equal opportunities) in the second year of the plan will complement new work on citizenship and environmental education. Improving links between the school and local business and industry (in which the governors will play a key role) will be a root to later curriculum development on economic and industrial understanding in the third year.

The school is already engaged in a local project on Records of Achievement, and this is to continue alongside work on the assessment implications of the National Curriculum.

Attendance emerged from the audit as an urgent priority, and the development of a better school policy on this is to be linked to improving the PSE programme.

Staff development is seen as a key root priority and therefore urgent. Although there were many other possible priorities meriting a place in the three-year plan, it has

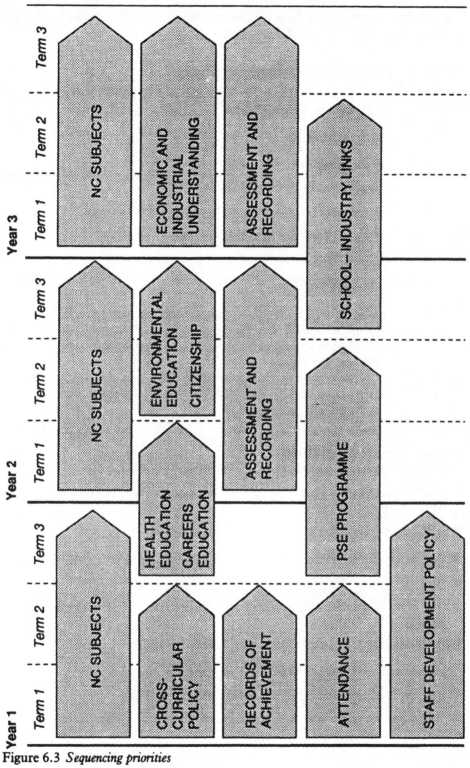

Figure 6.3 *Sequencing priorities*

been decided to leave 'spaces' for revision of the plan at the end of the first year to take account of experience and possible new demands.

WRITING UP AND PUBLICIZING THE PLAN

Once the plan is approved by the governors, it should be written up in a booklet of perhaps four to six pages and might include:

- the aims of the school;
- a review of the previous year's plan;
- the proposed priorities and their time-scale;
- the justification of the priorities in the context of the school;
- how the plan draws together different aspects of planning;
- the methods of reporting outcomes;
- the resource implications.

There are advantages in making the development plan widely available. Some schools display the plan in the staff room. Informing parents through the school newsletter or through a small booklet is desirable. Explaining the priorities and targets to pupils encourages their active involvement.

A summary of the process of plan construction is given on a step-by-step basis in Figure 6.4. The next stage, turning the priorities chosen for the first year of the plan into action plans, is explained in Chapter 7.

CHECKLIST OF QUESTIONS

- How and when are national and LEA policies and initiatives to be included?
- Which issues arising from the audit are to be included and how do they relate to external initiatives?
- Do the priorities further the fundamental aims of the school?
- How widely have the school's partners been consulted during plan construction?
- Has the full range of issues affecting choice been considered?
- Has careful thought been given to the quality of the school's 'roots' for sustaining the chosen priorities?
- Who will be responsible for what during the construction phase?
- Does everyone understand how the priorities will be decided?
- Does the development plan encompass other aspects of planning?
- Has the plan been sufficiently well publicized so that everyone knows about it?

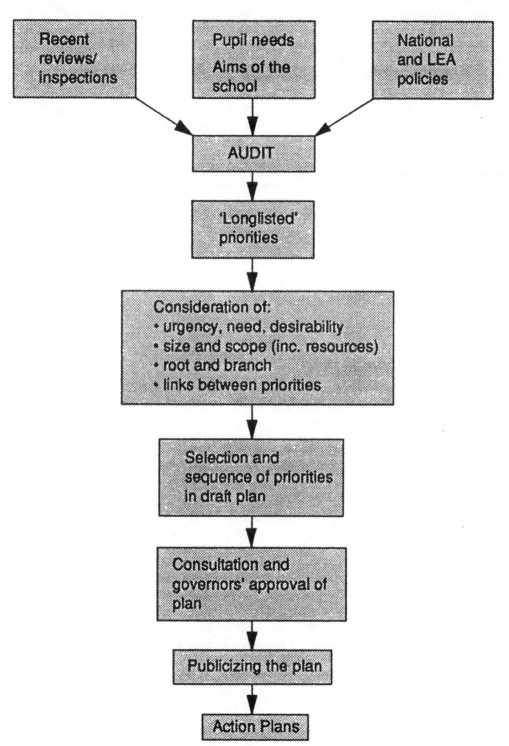

Figure 6.4 *The construction of the development plan*

Chapter 7

From Development Plan to Action Plans

Once the development plan as a whole has been agreed, the first year of the plan needs to be turned into a set of detailed *action plans* for each priority. These are the working documents for teachers. This chapter gives advice on how to construct action plans as an aid to effective implementation and evaluation. The main sections of the chapter are:

- What is an action plan?

- Drawing up the action plan.

- Illustrations of action plans.

WHAT IS AN ACTION PLAN?

An action plan is a working document which describes and summarizes what needs to be done to implement and evaluate a priority. It serves as a guide to implementation and helps to monitor progress and success.

Each priority is handed to a team or group who take responsibilities for the action plan. Every member of staff should be involved in at least one such team to ensure that everyone has a stake in the development plan as a whole. The workload needs to be distributed among the staff in such a way that no one is excluded, but that no one is overloaded. When individual workloads are aggregated, it underlines our earlier point that a school cannot take on too many priorities in any one year.

Each priority is turned into a series of targets. A *target* is a concrete objective or outcome within the priority. It clarifies what action needs to be taken in a particular school. A target is both a guide to immediate action and a focus for later evaluation. Schools may well have similar priorities, but the targets that comprise the priority will vary according to the individual circumstances of each school.

Each target can then be turned into a set of more discrete *tasks*, for which one or more members of the team will be responsible. The tasks as a whole represent the work involved in reaching the target and how it is to be shared among team members.

Targets must specify the criteria by which success in reaching the target can be judged, both by team members and by others. These *success criteria* are a form of school-generated performance indicator, which:

- give *clarity* about the target: what exactly are you trying to achieve?

- point to the *standard* expected by the team;

- provide advance warning of the *evidence* needed to judge successful implementation;

- give an indication of the *time-scale* involved.

The success criteria are a means for evaluating the outcomes of the plan, as well as providing benchmarks for development.

Teachers often find defining the success criteria the most difficult part of the action plan. It is much easier to break down a priority into targets and tasks than it is to define success criteria. Success criteria and performance indicators (Resource File 9) help the school to answer the fundamental question: has the quality of provision or practice improved as a result of the work on the priority? It is important that they specify the minimal acceptable standard, though the team will usually have aspirations to a standard of outcome which is much higher than this.

The main components of an action plan can be represented schematically as in Figure 7.1.

Each *action plan* describes, preferably on one side of A4, the programme of work to be undertaken. It contains:

- the *priority* as described in the development plan;

- the *targets*, or the more specific objectives for the priority;

- the *success criteria* against which progress and success on reaching targets can be judged;

- the *tasks* or work to be undertaken to reach each target (these may be attached as an appendix): there are tasks for both implementation and evaluation;

- the *allocation of responsibility* for targets and tasks, with time-lines;

- the dates for meetings *to assess progress*;

- the *resource* implications (e.g. materials and equipment, finance, INSET).

The action plan is thus a convenient summary of and guide to action.

The better the quality of the action plan, the more likely it is that implementation will proceed smoothly and successfully. It is therefore worth making time for the thought and discussion necessary to construct an action plan of good quality.

Work on a priority may take from one term to several years. As with any complicated journey or expedition, it is wise to plan as carefully as possible in advance. The action plan involves *preparations* for the journey; a road-map of the *routes* to be followed; and the *destinations* to be reached.

DRAWING UP THE ACTION PLAN

The team given the responsibility for drawing up the action plan meets and discusses what is involved in implementing the priority. The team needs to think at this point

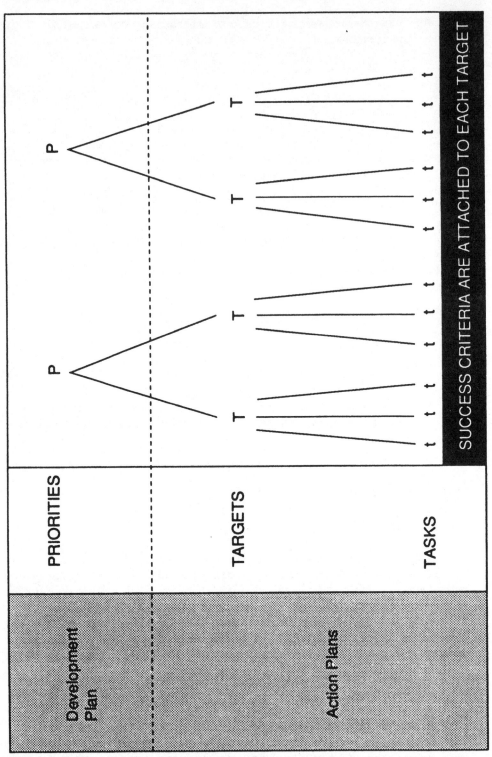

Figure 7.1 *The development plan and action plans*

about the programme of implementation over succeeding months so that the action plan becomes a practical guide planned in advance, rather than a vague statement of intentions. Figure 7.2 is designed to help the team to look ahead in a systematic way in order to provide the basis of a sound action plan.

The first step is to consider the question: what are the destinations of the journey of implementation? The *destinations* are the targets. Success criteria are much easier to set once targets have been framed in a provisional way. Thinking about the success criteria helps define the targets; thinking about the targets helps define the success criteria. Some talking through is often necessary to ensure the right 'fit' between success criteria and targets; either or both may need adjustment.

Once the targets and success criteria have been defined in this provisional way, the team then moves on to planning the *routes* to destinations. The targets are broken down into concrete tasks for groups or individuals within a chosen time-scale.

Progress checks need to be planned at the same time. They are designed to take place at regular points during implementation, usually at team meetings. They always pose a more specific version of the general question: how is it going so far? Progress checks allow the team to assess the extent to which tasks are being completed, standards are being met and the planned time-schedules are being observed. This is the least predictable part of the journey of implementation, so planning has to be at its most flexible to allow for modifications which might need to be made *en route*.

Once the destinations and routes have been sketched in outline, the team considers the initial tasks of making *preparations* for the journey: the basic requirements needed to carry the work forward. The resources, such as finance, materials and INSET, must be on hand or planned to be in place at the appropriate time.

The team can now finalize the action plan for the journey as a whole. The team drafts the action plan in the time-sequence appropriate to implementation (see Figure 7.3).

TWO ILLUSTRATIONS OF ACTION PLANNING

Action Planning at a Primary School

The primary school in Figure 6.2 took home–school partnership as one of its priorities. As the school is a three-teacher rural primary school, the action plan was drawn up by the whole staff at an after-school meeting.

The team decided that the head (Mrs Morgan) should not act as team leader for this priority and Mrs Green accepted the role. Mr Robinson suggested that the priority 'to improve our partnership with parents' was so global that it would take many years to implement in full. It was therefore agreed that the targets for the first year should be seen as the initial steps of a continuing programme of work. The targets must, however, be very specific and not cosmetic.

Mrs Morgan felt the partnership should be focused on children's achievement to avoid seeing partnership as 'cheese and wine parties' and said it should be linked with known parental concern about the impact of the National Curriculum and the school's recent work on language. The targets should therefore be a vehicle both for improving home–school relations and for meeting immediate school needs in enhancing pupils' reading skills within National Curriculum requirements.

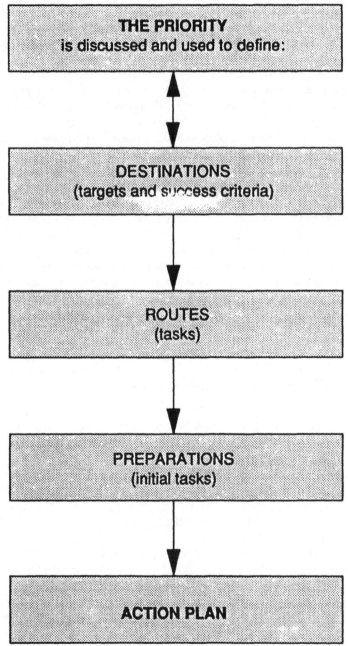

Figure 7.2 *The process of constructing an action plan*

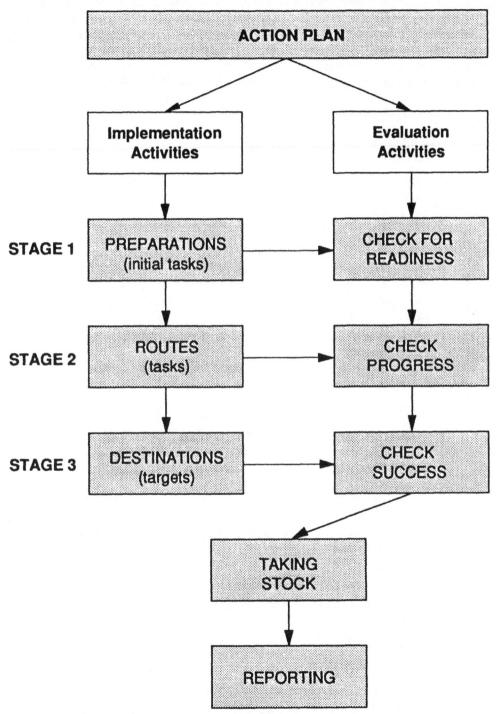

Figure 7.3 *Stages in implementing an action plan*

Mrs Green felt that they knew too little about parents' views on greater involvement in the work of the school, so it was agreed that the *first target* should be a survey of parental views. Mr Robinson suggested a questionnaire for parents, but this seemed very formal and some parents might not respond. A meeting for parents was proposed, but again parents might not attend and the topic was too vague to attract many parents. It was decided that parents' views could best be ascertained in informal ways, during their visits to the school or at the school gates. The team realized that this would be difficult to do systematically, so they enlisted the help of the school secretary and the Education Welfare Officer who often met parents when staff did not.

After discussion, it was agreed to ask parents for their views on three topics:

- Whether they would like to join in a class activity and when they would be available to do so.

- What they would like in the way of social events, meetings and curriculum workshops.

- What contribution parents felt they could make, at home, to their child's education, especially on reading, and how teachers might help and support this.

This would be the first target. It should take one term to complete. Parent-governors would assist in planning.

The *second target* would be to develop a home–school reading policy as an extension to work already completed on the language policy. Target two would also require:

- a special newsletter to parents on the language aspects of the National Curriculum, and the role they could play through reading to children and listening to their reading at home as part of the policy;

- a review of the school stock of books suitable for home reading.

The *third target*, the most important, would be the involvement of parents in reading. This would entail:

- 'workshops' for parents (separately for each of the three classes). In each class there would be one workshop during the day and one in the evening. As far as possible the day workshop would be fitted into normal classroom activities. The school's adviser and parent-governors would help with the design of these as well as in the events themselves if possible;

- a 'book fair' to which a bookseller or publisher and the local library would contribute to encourage parents to buy and borrow books in addition to those available from the school;

Box 7.1 *Action plan for home–school partnership*

Priority: To improve the school's partnership with parents and to devise a home–school reading scheme.

Target 1: Survey of parents' views during first term.

Success criteria: (a) number of parents responding: (b) quality of the response to each of the three main issues in the survey (details to be decided after questions are framed).

Target 2: Write policy for home–school reading, inform parents of it through newsletter and review book stock, also in first term if possible.

Success criteria: (a) adviser to judge quality of policy; (b) judgement of parent-governors and reaction of parents to newsletter; (c) review of stock to be defined during the activity.

Target 3: Involvement of parents in the workshops and book fair and in the home–school reading scheme; publication of articles in local newspaper (second or third term, depending on progress).

Success criteria: (a) attendance of parents and their response to the workshops and book fair; (b) changes in parental behaviour judged by borrowing of books and pupils' reports on home reading; (c) changes in pupil attitudes to reading judged by observation and increase in reading skills; (d) more community involvement in reading judged by comments to staff and parent governors.

Time: three terms.

Dates: (a) for progress checks – by all at each meeting; (b) for success checks – by Mrs Green as appropriate.

Resources: (a) money for new book stock; (b) cards to record parents' views as they are collected; (c) money for special edition of newsletter; (d) resources for the workshops and book fair.

Co-ordinator: Mrs Green.

Box 7.2 *Aide-mémoire on tasks for home–school partnership priority*

1 **Preparations** (initial tasks)
   a contact parent-governors to discuss the priority and obtain support (Mrs Green);
   b contact adviser for her views and active support in the book fair and workshops (Mrs Morgan);
   c obtain support of school secretary and Education Welfare Officer (Mrs Morgan).

2 **Routes** (tasks)
   a draw up questions for parents (Mr Robinson);
   b design cards for recording parent views (Mr Robinson);
   c check on whether all parents involved in the survey (Mrs Morgan with school secretary);
   d frame success criteria for judging quality of response to survey (Mrs Green);
   e draft policy for home–school reading (Mrs Green);
   f arrange discussion of policy with parent-governors and colleagues (Mrs Green);
   g discuss quality of policy with adviser (Mrs Morgan);
   h prepare newsletter (Mr Robinson with a parent-governor);
   i review book stock (all);
   j decide criteria for new stock (all);
   k plan workshops (Mrs Green);
   l plan book fair (Mr Robinson);
   m run workshops and book fair (all);
   n prepare extracts from newsletter for publication in local newspaper (a parent-governor);
   o check attendance and parents' reactions to these events (all);
   p observe pupils' attitudes to reading (all);
   q record extent of book borrowing (all);
   r ask pupils about home reading (all);
   s check changes in reading levels (all);
   t collate evidence from (p), (q) and (r) (Mrs Green).

3 **Destinations** (targets)
For targets – see Action Plan.
Final report: Mrs Green. (The final report would also contain suggestions on possible next steps in home–school partnership arising from the survey.)

- a series of articles in the local paper extolling the virtues of home reading and mentioning suitable books.

The team then considered the success criteria for each target. For the first target a key criterion would be quantitative: how many parents responded to their informal questions about their views. More important would be the *quality* of their response. This indicated that the questions would need careful thought: they would have to be designed to be important and relevant to parents; they would have to be framed in a way that parents felt pleased to be asked and they would have to win support for greater involvement in the school as well as providing information for staff. As Mrs Morgan observed, 'How we ask is as important as what we ask.'

For target two, the adviser would judge the quality of the home–school reading scheme. The quality of the newsletter would be judged by parent-governors and the reaction of parents. A short discussion about the criteria for reviewing and improving the book stock indicated that more time was needed for this. Success criteria for this would be devised during the task itself: the adviser might be able to help here. The success criteria for the workshops and book fair would be:

- the level of attendance and response of parents;

- subsequent changes in parental behaviour – borrowing of books and the extent of home reading: evidence to be drawn from pupils' accounts during normal classroom activities;

- the impact on pupils' attitudes and skills in reading, judged by classroom observation and records. Before setting a specific target for improvement, a careful assessment of the present position would be needed to provide a baseline.

The team then drafted the action plan (see Box 7.1) and Mrs Green agreed to produce an *aide-mémoire* of tasks (see Box 7.2), with dates for completion.

Action Planning at a Secondary School

The secondary school in Figure 6.3 took *attendance* as one of the priorities in the first year. This priority was described as 'to improve pupil attendance in the school as a whole and especially among older pupils'. A senior and experienced member of staff was given co-ordinating and overall responsibility for this priority. Three other teachers agreed to join the working team, with one parent-governor.

Destinations At the first meeting the team considered *destinations* (stage 3) and devised three main targets and their success criteria:

- *Target 1*. Pupil attendance in the school, and especially among older pupils should improve by the end of the second term in the period allowed for the priority (two terms). *Success criterion*: the degree of improved attendance judged through an analysis of pupil attendance by year group and class compared with attendance during the previous term and the second term of the previous year.

- *Target 2.* There should be a written policy on attendance. *Success criterion*: the policy should be written by half-term of the first term.

- *Target 3.* The policy should command the support of teachers, parents and pupils. *Success criterion*: the degree to which the policy is accepted and in force by the end of the second term.

- The team recognized that target 1 was the main outcome to successful implementation and could be evaluated by 'hard' evidence. Targets 2 and 3 were the key to success but could be judged less easily: the evidence about the quality of the policy and the extent of its acceptance would need careful thought.

Routes   The team then turned their attention to *routes* (stage 2) and assigned tasks and progress checks to each target:

- *Target 2.* This was vital to progress and so was considered first. It was decided that to write a really good policy it would be desirable for a team member to attend a relevant INSET course and for all the team to visit a school with a similar intake, but better attendance, to discuss policy and practice. These two tasks would make the main task of actually drafting the policy easier as well as providing criteria by which the quality of the policy could be judged. Once these became clear they could be built into the success criteria for the target. It was also agreed to invite the school's inspector to comment on the quality of the policy in the light of her knowledge of policies in other schools. Dates for meetings to write the policy were agreed and progress checks for the three tasks planned.

- *Target 3.* To get the policy agreed there would be a need for a professional training day (part of which would include governors and parents) to discuss the draft. Formal adoption of the policy would take place at a subsequent governors' meeting and a staff meeting. The parent-governor offered to write an article commending the policy to parents in the school's newsletter. Teachers would explain and discuss the policy with pupils in their classes. It was suggested that pupils would be more likely to accept the policy if they contributed to the drafting, so this new task was added to target 2.

  The team leader raised the issue of gathering evidence on the success criteria. This was easily done on the target 'writing the policy': either it would be written on time or it would not. Staff acceptance would be more difficult to gauge. One team member suggested a survey of staff but that was rejected as being too cumbersome. Another suggested a vote at a staff meeting, but votes at staff meetings were generally avoided. The best suggestion was that each team member would talk to several named colleagues, over coffee during the week following the professional training day, to get their views on the policy. These views would be pooled at the next team meeting as a measure of staff acceptance. The best test of acceptance by pupils and parents would be the degree of improvement in attendance. If this did not occur, further attempts to assess acceptance would be needed.

Appropriate progress checks were then devised for each task. This drew attention to the need to schedule the tasks for target 2 with care as these were critical to the time-schedule of the priority as a whole.

- *Target 1*. This was then broken down into tasks. Data on attendance during the second term would need to be collated on a week-by-week basis to avoid a major task at the very end, and so the four teachers arranged to do this on a rota.

Preparations Finally, the team looked at the *preparations* (stage 1) and readiness checks.

- Evidence on the previous poor attendance had already been collected in the audit phase. Action would need to be taken to find an INSET course and to reserve a place; the school's inspector would need to be contacted to identify a school to visit and the head's agreement to the visit would be sought; the professional training day would need to be booked and planned; space in the newsletter for the parent-governor's article would also have to be booked.

- The teacher who acted as secretary to the team then agreed to record in the minutes a short summary of the plan in the right time-sequence of preparations, routes and destinations and from this would draw up the action plan (see Box 7.3). A copy would be given to the head who, after final approval, would add it to the collection of action plans for the development plan as a whole. An *aide-mémoire* of tasks (see Box 7.4) would help to maintain progress.

In this way the teams at the primary and secondary schools adopted different ways of constructing their action plans, but both:

- produced an action plan which was a practical guide (to action) because the whole journey had been thought through in advance;

- allowed evaluation, through the use of success criteria, to shape the process of implementation;

- planned for the collection of evaluative evidence *en route* so that the evaluation would not become a separate and time-consuming activity at the end of implementation.

Box 7.3 *Action plan for attendance priority*

Priority: To improve pupil attendance in the school especially among older pupils.

Target 1: Improve attendance in second term of implementation of the priority.

Success criterion: quantify degree of improvement by comparison with previous attendance records.

Target 2: Produce a written policy by half-term of first term of implementation.

Success criteria: (a) meeting of time-schedule; (b) quality of policy to be judged on criteria to be determined later.

Target 3: Policy should command support of teachers, parents and pupils.

Success criterion: degree of acceptance by teachers, parents and pupils of the new policy.

Time: two terms.

Dates: (a) for progress checks – by all at each team meeting; (b) for success checks – by Ms Smith at end of second term.

Resources: (a) an INSET course for one team member; (b) time for visit to another school; (c) a professional training day; (d) space in newsletter to parents.

Team Leader: Ms Smith (who has a detailed note on the tasks involved).

Team Members: Mr Jones, Mrs Davies, Mr Brown and Mrs Thomas (parent-governor).

Box 7.4 *Aide-mémoire tasks for attendance priority*

1 **Preparations** (initial tasks)
  a   book and attend INSET course (Ms Smith);
  b   contact inspector to identify school for visit and make arrangements for visit (Mr Jones);
  c   book and plan professional training day (Mrs Brown);
  d   plan space in newsletter (Mrs Thomas).

2 **Routes** (tasks)
  a   visit school (as many as available);
  b   decide success criteria on quality of policy (all);
  c   draft policy (Ms Smith to take load);
  d   obtain inspector view on its quality (Mr Jones);
  e   professional training day (Ms Smith and Mrs Brown);
  f   check acceptance of policy (all);
  g   present policy to governors (Mrs Thomas);
  h   present policy to staff (Ms Smith);
  i   present policy to pupils (all staff – briefed by Mrs Brown);
  j   write article in newsletter (Mrs Thomas);
  k   gain support to implement policy (all);
  l   collect evidence on attendance (all – by rota);
  m collate evidence and make comparison with previous attendance records (Mrs Davies).

3 **Destinations** (targets)
For targets – see Action Plan.
Final report: Ms Smith and Mrs Davies.

A systematic approach to action planning improves teachers' skills and the quality of their professional judgement.

CHECKLIST OF QUESTIONS

- Has each priority been turned into a set of targets?

- Is there a team leader for every target?

- Are there tasks for every teacher?

- Is anyone overloaded?

- Are there clear success criteria, both quantitative and qualitative, for each target?

- Do the tasks relate to both implementation and evaluation?

- Are the initial/preparatory tasks distinct?

- Are the expectations and time-lines clear and agreed?

- Have the resource implications been assessed?

- Have all possible sources of help and support to implement the action plan been identified?

- Is it clear who is to report on the success of the action plan?

Chapter 8

Making the Development Plan Work

It is much easier to construct a development plan than to implement it successfully and to produce evidence of success. Many existing guidelines on school development planning describe implementation and evaluation as separate stages or phases. In some regards this is sensible: one cannot truly check on whether targets have been met until after implementation. The risk, however, is that schools may begin to ask themselves basic questions about evaluation late in their planning and so run into three problems:

- Evaluating progress becomes difficult because the preparatory groundwork has been neglected.

- The teachers find they have too little time to undertake evaluation.

- Because it has been left too late, evaluation cannot support implementation.

To help schools to avoid these problems, we treat the processes of implementation and evaluation as interlaced, not as a period of implementation followed by a 'big bang' evaluation at the end. If implementation and evaluation are linked, evaluation can help to shape and guide the action plan rather than being a post-mortem upon it.

A well-prepared action plan uses the success criteria and progress checks to build evaluation activities into the process of implementation. This chapter shows how implementation and evaluation are linked when the action plans are put into practice.

Implementing the action plan involves:

- sustaining commitment during implementation;

- checking the progress of implementation;

- overcoming any problems encountered;

- checking the success of implementation;

- taking stock;

- reporting progress;

- constructing the next development plan.

Figure 8.1, which is an elaboration of Figure 1.1, illustrates this. The rest of this chapter explains the steps taken during implementation and evaluation.

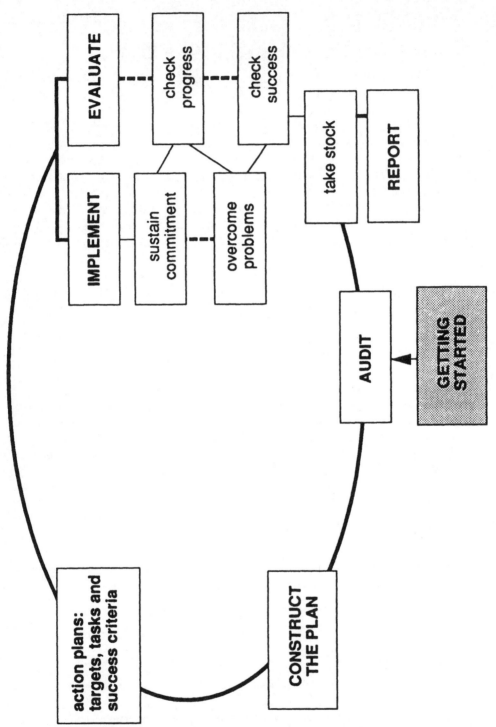

Figure 8.1 *The development planning process*

SUSTAINING COMMITMENT DURING IMPLEMENTATION

After the work of audit and construction, it is easy for the head and senior staff to assume that an action plan, once agreed, will somehow look after itself. Yet experience suggests that *implementation does not proceed on automatic pilot*.

Successful implementation needs continual support. Sustaining commitment is a key task for the head, senior staff and team leaders. The enthusiasm of even the most committed staff can flag when routine work and unanticipated events distract teachers from the action plan.

Senior staff can boost motivation and so sustain commitment by:

- *showing interest*. An occasional, informal enquiry about progress to a teacher or team demonstrates that their efforts are being appreciated and provides an opportunity for reporting difficulties.

- *making themselves accessible*. Many teachers are reluctant to encroach on the time of the head or senior staff, who need to make it clear that they are available for staff to talk through progress and problems.

- *joining meetings*. Senior staff should occasionally join team meetings since they may be able to provide help, especially if outside assistance (e.g. from an LEA officer) is needed.

CHECKING THE PROGRESS OF IMPLEMENTATION

A *progress check* is an act of evaluation *in the course of* implementation. It is a response to the question: how are we doing so far? Many progress checks are intuitive, a 'feel' for whether things are going well or badly. This is a natural part of monitoring one's activities: it becomes more systematic if these intuitive reactions are shared within the team.

At least once a term progress should be formally checked for each task against the success criteria associated with the target (see Figure 8.2). The team will need some clear *evidence* of the extent of progress: if such evidence is recorded, the workload at a later stage will be reduced.

Regular *progress checks* involve:

- giving somebody in the team responsibility for ensuring that the progress checks take place;

- reviewing progress at team meetings, especially when taking the next step forward or making decisions about future directions;

- deciding what will count as evidence of progress in relation to the success criteria;

- finding quick methods of collecting evidence from different sources;

- recording the evidence and conclusions for later use.

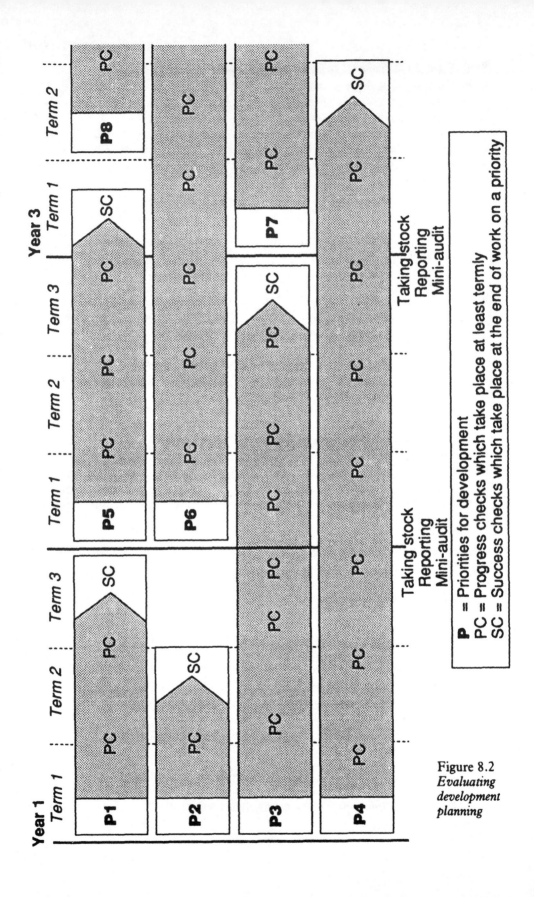

Figure 8.2
*Evaluating
development
planning*

OVERCOMING ANY PROBLEMS ENCOUNTERED

Some progress checks may show that:

- the time schedules were too tight;

- circumstances have changed since the plan was constructed and unexpected obstacles have been encountered;

- there is a loss of direction and some mid-course correction is required for the target to be met.

Implementing the action plan can be a hazardous journey – a bit like snakes and ladders. Progress proceeds in fits and starts. Progress checks provide a pause when re-orientation can take place. What may appear to be a major set-back, e.g. the loss of a senior or key member of staff, can often be overcome. Useful tactics include:

- providing extra support to the affected team;

- re-assigning roles and responsibilities within the team;

- drawing upon the skills and experience of new members of staff;

- seeking additional outside help;

- 'freezing' temporarily part of the action plan, thus making sure no ground is lost whilst awaiting better circumstances;

- modifying the projected time-scale;

- scaling down the planned action to more manageable proportions;

- postponing a target to a later year and bringing forward a substitute target.

Circumstances may also change for the better and advantage can be taken of unforeseen opportunities to advance the rate of progress.

CHECKING THE SUCCESS OF IMPLEMENTATION

Success checks take place at the end of the developmental work on a target. The team now decides how successful the implementation of the target or priority as a whole has been. Checking success need not be complex or time-consuming. It will consist largely in collating, and then drawing a conclusion about, the earlier progress checks.

A *success check* means:

- giving somebody responsibility for collating the progress checks;

- allowing time for the team to discuss and analyse the extent of the success;

- noting changes in practice as a result of the plan;

- writing a brief report on target implementation;

- collating the reports on each of the targets to create a final report on the priority as a whole with indications of what helped and what hindered progress;

- working out the implications for future work;

- assessing the implications for all those not involved in the implementation and for the school as a whole.

TAKING STOCK

This takes place at the end of each planning cycle. In essence, taking stock is a collation and brief analysis of reports on each of the priorities – both progress checks and, where the priority has been completed, success checks. This is the most formal evaluation activity of the school year and should be co-ordinated by a senior member of staff.

Different priorities and targets have different time-scales as seen in Figure 8.2. Some will be completed during the year; others last for more than a year. There is no single point in the school's calendar that is exclusively concerned with evaluation. Taking stock is the point when the school checks the success about completed priorities and assesses progress for priorities which are implemented in part.

The purpose of *taking stock* is to:

- examine the progress and success of the implementation of the plan;

- assess the extent to which the school's aims have been furthered;

- assess the impact of the plan on pupils' learning and achievement;

- decide how to disseminate successful new practices throughout the school;

- make the process of reporting easier.

REPORTING PROGRESS

Taking stock provides the basis on which the head can make an annual progress report to the governing body.

Governors will know about the outcomes of the plan through their visits to the school and through the head's regular reports.

Parents may be informed at the annual parents' meeting, through a newsletter or at an open day.

Reporting to *pupils* should not be forgotten. They play an active role in implementing the plan and have an interest in the outcomes.

CONSTRUCTING THE NEXT DEVELOPMENT PLAN

After taking stock and reporting on progress, the school prepares the next three-year development plan.

The priorities for the second year of the original plan should now become the priorities for the first year of the new plan. This cannot be done in any mechanical

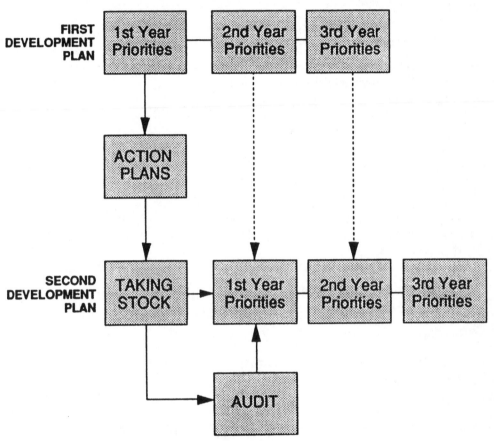

Figure 8.3 *Constructing the next development plan*

way. The content of the new development plan, especially .the first year, will be shaped by other factors, such as:

- any lessons learnt from taking stock on the implementation of the original plan;

- the outcomes of the school's annual audit of curriculum and resources;

- the outcomes of any specific audit undertaken as part of the school's rolling programme of audits;

- changes in national and local policies and initiatives;

- the changing needs and circumstances of the school;

- any slow-down or acceleration in progress.

The process is summarized in Figure 8.3.

In practice, it is usually easier and less time-consuming to construct the second development plan, partly because everyone has gained some experience of plan construction and partly because the second plan has already been to some degree shaped by the original plan.

CHECKLIST OF QUESTIONS

- How do the senior staff actively support implementation?

- Have progress checks been carried out for each target?

- How do the results of progress checks help to overcome problems?

- Who is responsible for success checks?

- How does taking stock aid the construction of next year's plan?

- Do the reporting procedures include all those involved and interested?

Chapter 9

Enhancing Professional Judgement

Development planning requires teachers to use their professional judgement in a systematic way to evaluate progress. This chapter explores how teachers can evaluate development planning in ways that enhance their skills.

USING AN INTUITIVE PROFESSIONAL JUDGEMENT

Teachers already, as part of their everyday activities, monitor and evaluate their own actions as well as the behaviour and work of pupils. This skill, as every student teacher or new teacher knows, is not easily acquired. Constant monitoring and evaluation of oneself and one's pupils, especially in the busy world of the classroom, is initially a rather deliberate activity. With experience, it can be undertaken quickly, almost automatically. Teachers acquire the skill of making an intuitive appreciation of what is going well or badly and of how they should respond. From the multitude of classroom events they monitor, teachers learn to pick out key events and make an almost instant decision on how they should be handled.

If teachers did not rely upon their *intuitive professional judgement*, they would not be able to cope with the complexities of their work. There are occasions, however, when it cannot be wholly relied upon as a basis for making a decision. Such occasions are when:

- teachers are not entirely confident about their intuitive judgement;

- the issue is of considerable importance or significance.

In these circumstances, teachers make a *considered professional judgement*, which requires some action to check the intuitive judgement.

MAKING A CONSIDERED PROFESSIONAL JUDGEMENT

A considered professional judgement is reached by:

- further investigation;

- reflection.

A teacher may judge intuitively that a particular pupil is not making adequate progress. Further investigation follows: a check on the pupil's written work over a period of time; a review of the record of marks; close observation of the pupil in class; and a discussion with the pupil. Through reflection on the evidence and on possible courses of action, the teacher decides what to do.

Using intuitive and considered professional judgements is a routine part of being a teacher. Both are a natural and inherent part of evaluating progress and success in the implementation of a development plan. However, innovations create new working circumstances with which the teacher is less familiar; and since the teacher wants the innovation to succeed, there may be a bias towards noticing the most favourable evidence. Professional judgement may therefore be less trustworthy than usual.

Development planning depends upon an accurate and honest evaluation of progress and success. It *requires* a refined professional judgement and at the same time presents an *opportunity* for enhancing professional judgement.

REFINING PROFESSIONAL JUDGEMENTS
This is done through:

- *discussion with others*, such as colleagues or the school's partners, about the extent of progress or success in implementing a priority. Other people's perceptions may confirm one's professional judgement, or they may differ from it, in which case the grounds of the judgement may need to be questioned and talked through. A discussion of progress at regular team meetings is a formal opportunity for sharing professional judgements and their basis.

- establishing *agreement on standards*. Differences in judgements about the extent of progress or success may reflect differences in the standards being applied. Development planning is concerned with *improvements* of various kinds: but *from what* and *to what* is the improvement to be judged? Different conclusions about progress and success, either between teachers or between teachers and others, sometimes arise from a lack of clarity about the state of affairs in the school *before* the priority is implemented. Careful auditing helps to avoid this problem.

  In the same way, standards about the expected *outcomes* of implementing the plan can be a source of disagreement. For some, yardsticks of progress or success may be based on a comparison with previous practice in the school, whilst others may use an external point of comparison, such as the standard being achieved in another school or the standard set by other people, such as inspectors.

  When the success criteria for a priority have been carefully specified, the possibility of such disagreements about standards of progress or success is reduced. Development planning heightens everybody's awareness of standards, what is meant by them and how their achievement is to be evaluated.

- *mutual observation* in the classroom. When teachers observe one another, as part of a team approach to teaching or as an aspect of teacher appraisal, they are enabled to share also the ways in which professional judgements are made and the grounds for them. Provided that the relationship is characterized by mutual trust and support, the professional judgement of both teachers can be extended.

- the use of *informed opinion*. Reading accounts of other teachers' experiences, HMI reports, LEA documents, research studies or books and journals on education extends teachers' understanding and refines professional judgement, especially when such material is used to reflect upon one's own practice.

In short, development planning provides ample opportunities for teachers to talk with others, to seek agreement on standards, to observe one another and to read relevant documentation: all are means of extending the professional judgements which are essential to evaluation.

COMPLEMENTING PROFESSIONAL JUDGEMENTS WITH EVIDENCE

There are circumstances when teachers need to complement even considered professional judgements with additional *evidence*. Such occasions are when:

- others need to be persuaded of the validity of teachers' judgements;
- when there are benefits to all if teachers' judgements are backed by independent evidence.

The basis for evaluating how far targets and success criteria are met will often consist of a mixture of professional judgements and complementary evidence. Collecting complementary evidence is usually more time-consuming than making professional judgements, so careful thought needs to be given to:

- what kind of complementary evidence is appropriate to documenting success;
- how it can be collected as quickly and easily as possible without adding substantially to existing workloads.

In collecting evidence, staff should consider *qualitative* information, such as views, opinions and judgements, as well as *quantitative* information in the form of statistics. Both kinds of evidence are very important. The distinction between the two types of information is not a sharp one – counting views transforms qualitative opinions into a quantitative summary of perceptions. The strength of the evidence comes from using a range of sources which helps cross-checking before conclusions are reached.

There are different types and sources of complementary evidence:

- *observations*. Observation of pupils at work and around the school is already part of making routine professional judgements. Where a development priority is concerned with pupil work and behaviour, there may be a need to make these observations more *methodical and systematic* on a selective basis and to make a brief record of them.

Such records or diaries, considered in reflection at a later stage, provide powerful complementary evidence to support teacher judgements about the kind, extent and quality of changes in pupils.

Mutual observation by teachers, if objective data are briefly recorded, provides independent evidence on a priority such as changing teaching styles or improving questioning techniques. At the same time, by providing a basis for discussion, it helps to refine teachers' professional judgements on their own behaviour.

- *views and opinions*. Discussion with others has been noted as a way of extending professional judgement. If the views and opinions are recorded, in the form of a summary of a discussion or through a short questionnaire, relevant evidence is easily obtained. The written views of LEA officers can be useful here.

  Pupils have views and knowledge which are not always explicitly available. If they are asked formally for their opinions about, or reactions to, a priority which affects them (by means of discussion, a piece of written work, a review sheet or a brief questionnaire), they usually respond constructively and provide insights into their experience. Documenting the pupils' response to changes is one of the most valuable forms of evidence.

- *written materials*. Two important sources of complementary evidence are teachers' records and pupils' work. A detailed study of records over time can help to detect and document changes which might otherwise be overlooked, as well as suggesting better ways of keeping records. A 'book-look', where samples of pupils' books are examined by a small group of staff, can be used to review the impact of a curriculum change or of a newly devised policy on assessment and marking.

- *statistical information*. Schools collect much statistical information already, both for their own use and for the LEA and other agencies. This can also be drawn upon as complementary evidence relevant to development planning. Trends in pupil attendance rates (and differences between year groups) provide vital evidence where attendance is a development priority. New documentation on curriculum provision is now required and serves as evidence on the implementation of the National Curriculum.

- *more formal research*. In many schools, one or more members of staff are following INSET courses or taking diplomas and degrees in higher education. Course work, dissertations and informal groups provide a basis for 'action research' by which teachers research and document the progress and outcomes of a part of the development plan. This contributes to the teacher's professional development and also helps the school to generate complementary evidence of the highest quality.

Enhancing teachers' professional judgements:

- makes it easier to report fully to governors, parents and the LEA on the outcomes of the development plan;

- provides ways of linking the school's internal monitoring and evaluation with the monitoring and evaluation of the LEA officers;

- links the professional development of the individual teacher to the development of the school as a whole;

- improves the quality of teaching and learning.

CHECKLIST OF QUESTIONS

- How far are teachers' professional judgements included in the evaluation of the development plan?

- Are there opportunities provided for teachers to refine their professional judgements?

- How often are professional judgements complemented with *additional* evidence in the evaluation of the plan?

- How is evidence used to support judgements made about development planning?

ACTIVITY

- Examine the action plans set out in Chapter 7 and consider how the teachers, in executing these plans, were able to enhance their professional judgements.

Chapter 10

The School Moves On

For many schools, the experience of development planning is still relatively new. Sometimes it has been the LEA which took the initiative, often requiring schools to submit a plan with the support of officers and published guidelines, but frequently within a short time-scale. Sometimes it has been the school's own initiative, after hearing about development planning from various sources, including this project's booklet *Planning for School Development*.

For some teachers, it has been just one more demand upon their time and energy, involving yet more meetings and paperwork. For others, it has been a welcome support to managing and controlling the pace of change: an additional demand certainly, but one which is worth the effort.

Most schools find it relatively easy to produce a written plan. The *process* of creating a workable plan which can be implemented and evaluated to the real benefit of the school often proves to be more troublesome. Obstacles are inevitably encountered and some mistakes are made.

Through such experiences each school discovers for itself that development planning is not a simple matter of following some mistake-proof recipe, but a process of *learning*. Often it takes a school two or three years of development planning before the full benefits are felt. As planning cycles succeed one another, the implementation and evaluation of change become easier as skills are enhanced.

Schools become progressively aware of three main gains from their learning.

THE OUTCOMES OF PLANNING

There are real outcomes to development planning, the most important of which affect pupils' learning and achievement. But apart from the successful implementation, in whole or in part, of specific priorities, schools recognize unexpected dividends among the outcomes:

- improved understanding, communication and co-operation among governors, head and staff and the school's partners;

- better staff development which links individual professional development with institutional improvement;

- a raising of expectations about what ought to be achieved and what can be achieved;

- a growing commitment to improving the quality of teaching and learning;

- greater confidence of governors, head and staff and of the school's partners in the work of the school.

THE ENHANCEMENT OF EXPERTISE

Through the process of development planning, governors, head and staff acquire or improve their skills, including the capacity to:

- recognize and build on strengths;

- assess and remedy limitations;

- plan and execute change by manageable steps;

- devise systems of quality assurance that link accountability to school improvement;

- deploy the talents and dedication of all involved through collaboration.

THE REVITALIZATION OF THE SCHOOL'S CULTURE

Development planning transforms the culture of the school by:

- promoting a shared vision for the school;

- creating management arrangements that empower;

- providing for every teacher a role in the management of the school and opportunities for leadership;

- encouraging everyone involved to have a stake in the school's continuing improvement;

- generating the commitment and confidence which springs from success.

Over time, the creation of such a culture is both an indicator and a test of the quality of development planning, the purpose of which is the well-managed school with confident teachers who know that their pupils attain the highest standards of achievement.

PART THREE

ORGANIZATION AND SUPPORT

Chapter 11

Diagnosing Difficulties in Development Planning

This book, like most guidelines on school development plans, consists of a recipe of advice which, if followed sensibly and creatively, should help a school to achieve its aims and manage change successfully.

In practice, some schools respond to the advice as intended, and find the advice helpful and relatively easy to put into effect. Other schools cannot or do not respond as expected; and yet, it is often precisely these schools which are in greatest need of this advice. The consequence is that the gap between the most and least effective schools tends to widen.

Why does this state of affairs arise and what can be done about it? It is evident that some schools are not in a state or condition to respond positively and effectively to advice on development planning. There is a need to clarify the problem and explore ways in which it can be overcome.

The best solutions require a partnership between schools and LEA officers. We believe that this chapter can contribute to a discussion among LEA officers, to a dialogue between a head and the school's adviser/inspector, and perhaps to a discussion within a school for which the advice given in Chapters 3 and 4 poses real problems.

We start from the discussion in Chapter 3 of the tension between development and maintenance, and how this tension is expressed in the school's culture through its choice of management arrangements. The school's response to development planning is a reflection of the culture that has come to characterize the school and the choices it has made about frameworks, roles and working together.

The existing culture and management arrangements seem to be a fact of life: how they came into being is complex. Their present nature is the product of choices and preferences made in the past, and sometimes the distant past, which have become established as the school's traditions, values and routine ways of working. Choices and preferences can be changed, but to do so requires some careful thought in relation to what the choices were about. We show eight areas in which every school has to make a choice (see Box 11.1). Taken together they represent a comprehensive description of the boundaries of a school's organization. None of the areas can be ignored: some kind of choice is inescapable. Once a choice has been made, this influences the school's culture and management arrangements. Moreover the choices tend to be linked to one another: there are patterns to the choices.

The choices made by schools show considerable variation. Each choice highlights the tension between development and maintenance. The choices can be understood as leaning towards either development or maintenance, or as falling between the two (see Figure 11.1), but there are obviously more than three variations. A *profile* could be

Box 11.1 *The choices all schools have to make*

Choice 1: Aims. Schools have aims (goals or purposes) which are multiple and diffuse. It is not at all clear what these aims are or should be, how they are to be achieved or how it can be shown that they have indeed been achieved.

Choice 2: Partners. There is confusion about whether the partners of the school (the government, the DES, the LEA, governors, the parents, the local community, pupils) are the groups who should determine what schools should do or are those who receive the school's services (as clients or consumers), or both. This confusion is greater than in other professional fields (e.g. medicine, law, architecture).

Choice 3: Curriculum. In recent years there has been growing confusion about the meaning of the school's curriculum. It can refer to the content of lessons in a very narrow sense, or it can be interpreted as the totality of the experience of pupils as they learn and develop, as a product of school, home and life in the community.

Choice 4: Organization. Everybody acknowledges that schools are centrally concerned with teaching and learning. But how teaching and learning should be organized is solved in widely different ways by the schools. That teachers should teach and pupils should learn does not in itself lead naturally or easily to agreed means of organizing these activities.

Choice 5: Management. Teaching and learning are only part of what is meant by school organization. Schools are complex organizations which adopt a wide variety of means to conduct their affairs. They devise such management arrangements to sustain their chosen form of organization.

Choice 6: Change. Change always challenges current assumptions and practices. Schools have to choose which changes to make and then devise strategies for implementing them in the interest of school improvement but without damage to existing good practice.

Choice 7: Support. Schools cannot survive, let alone develop and change, without support, if only from parents and pupils. At times of change, schools have to decide when and how to mobilize support to assist them.

Choice 8: Ethos. Schools develop an 'ethos' (climate or atmosphere). The notion is widely accepted: but what exactly is ethos and can it be created or changed?

Extreme development position

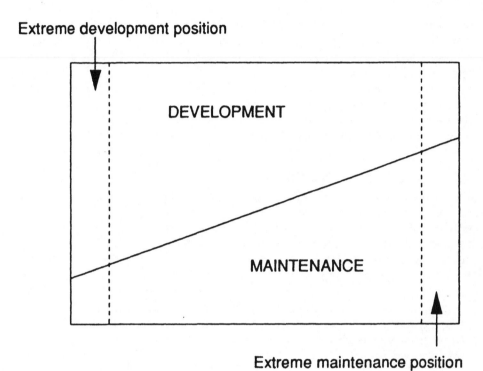

DEVELOPMENT

MAINTENANCE

Extreme maintenance position

Figure 11.1 *Responses to the choices*

drawn for any individual school (or part of a school) according to how it responds to each of the eight choices.

At the extremes the orientation is strongly towards either development or maintenance. A few schools will tend towards one of the extremes in a consistent way for all the eight choices; most schools have a more 'mixed' profile, at one or other extreme for some choices and in a more central position for other choices.

The purpose of this profile is to diagnose the nature of those difficulties which a school, or part of a school, is likely to experience with development planning. It is *not* intended as a measure of school quality or school effectiveness. Schools are judged by themselves or others as effective or successful on the basis of different criteria, and successful schools may have very different profiles in relation to the eight choices. Our research indicates that it is schools which have an overall profile tending consistently to one extreme which have the greatest problems with development planning; schools with a more mixed profile, or a profile which tends towards a central position, will (whatever the state of their effectiveness judged by other criteria) be more likely to respond favourably and successfully to development planning.

ILLUSTRATIONS OF CHOICES

The characterizations which follow are *illustrations* (for heuristic purposes) of the extreme positions and a more central position. If a school, or part of a school, leans too heavily towards development, it becomes so concerned with innovation that it becomes unstable by its neglect of continuity; if a school, or part of a school, leans too heavily towards maintenance, it is so concerned with preserving the status quo that it cannot respond to the need for change. Schools which have a mixed profile or tend towards a central position between the extremes are more favourable to development planning since they recognize the tension between development and maintenance. It is these schools which understand that they cannot innovate to the point where they damage the maintenance system but also that the maintenance system may inhibit the process of innovation.

Choice 1: Multiple and Diffuse Goals and Purposes

At the maintenance extreme, the school's aims are largely rhetorical and the school develops its own very different operational goals which may not reflect the needs of pupils or parents. At the development extreme, the school is constantly changing or refining its aims in the light of changing circumstances, but this creates discontinuity or lack of coherence. In the middle position, the multiple and diffuse nature of the aims is accepted, but at varying times attention is paid to how one or more aims should be considered in detail so that strategies can be developed to achieve them and to monitor and evaluate their achievement. However, it may not always innovate in an area where change is most needed, because a system for monitoring and evaluation is lacking.

Choice 2: The Role of Partners

At the maintenance extreme, the school emphasizes its autonomy, especially the professional autonomy of the teachers. Pressures from the school's partners are seen as unnecessary interference and as a lack of trust in the professionalism and existing achievements of the staff. At the development extreme, the school strives to be so responsive to all the partners that the school loses its sense of identity and internal consistency as it cannot resolve the sometimes conflicting expectations of different partners. Another version of the development extreme is that the school's main innovation direction is such that a key partner (the parents, the LEA) loses confidence in the school. In the middle position, the school recognizes these different expectations and strives, with variable degrees of success, to achieve a balance between responding to them and explaining the school's position on particular issues in a spirit of co-operative partnership.

Choice 3: The Curriculum

At the maintenance extreme, the school insists upon its own definition of the curriculum in terms of what the teachers teach. Outside pressures for curriculum change are seen as threatening. At the development extreme, groups of teachers conceive of the curriculum in widely different ways and seek to develop these different conceptions, leading to lack of consensus on curriculum matters. In the middle position, the school strives towards holistic or whole-school curriculum policies to bind the staff together. Curriculum change is seen to require a whole school response and strategy for implementation, but practice often falls short of this ideal.

Choice 4: The Organization of Teaching and Learning

At the maintenance extreme, teachers spend almost all their time teaching and do so in classrooms in professional isolation from their colleagues. Whatever the present form of organization, it is thought to be tried and tested and cannot be changed since this would disturb the autonomy of each teacher. Another version of this maintenance extreme is that the school is so totally committed to a particular form of organization (e.g. mixed ability/streaming; integrated studies/single subject teaching) that any innovation which challenges this is resisted. At the development extreme, new forms of organization are under constant consideration, but staff become divided about new forms of organization to which not all can subscribe. For schools in the middle position, changes in organization arise slowly after agreement on the basis of debate or the results of innovations piloted by a group of staff and then carefully evaluated. In practice, it proves difficult and slow to achieve such consensus on changes needed or the outcome of pilot schemes, and in some cases consensus is achieved only on issues of marginal importance.

Choice 5: School Management

At the maintenance extreme, the head and deputy are the 'management', and it is their job to manage, though the way they do so may incur dissent or resentment. There is confusion between management and administration. Leadership is a quality expected of the head. At the development extreme, every innovation and change leads to new roles and designations of responsibility, and there is confusion about who is responsible for what. In the middle position, there are clear lines of responsibility for those functions necessary for maintenance, but 'task groups' are created to implement new ideas which cut across the line-management. A spirit of collegiality exists alongside a structure for responsibility and accountability. Teachers share in the management of the school; leadership is a quality exercised by all staff, depending upon the circumstances. The head strives to be a supportive enabler, without abdicating responsibility for the school as a whole.

Choice 6: Innovation and Change

At the maintenance extreme, demands for change are seen as intrusive and potential sources of damage. If change cannot be resisted, each innovation is treated as a separate entity, affecting a limited area of the school and unrelated to the school's main work. The head leaves such innovations to individuals or groups; they tend to die when the innovating staff leave. At the development extreme, the head enthusiastically embraces individual innovations as they arrive, and some staff may consequently engage in so many innovations that they become overwhelmed by them. Innovations are rarely evaluated and the school's rhetoric about innovation is far in advance of its practice. Again, innovations tend not to survive the departure of their originators. In the middle position, the school builds innovation very selectively upon existing practice after collective deliberation. Innovation tends to survive the departure of the original key staff. The head finds time to support the innovations, but may not find it easy to cope with the increased pace of change and with innovations to which the staff are unsympathetic.

Choice 7: Support Systems

At the maintenance extreme, insufficient support is provided internally for an innovation, and little use is made of external support, e.g. from the officers, parents, governors, higher education. There is no policy for staff development. Teachers attend external courses for their own professional development rather than to meet the needs of the school. At the development extreme, teachers are so involved in highly diverse INSET that staff are frequently out of school and classes have many supply teachers. In the middle position, there is a staff development policy designed to support a limited range of innovation to meet the school's needs. Teachers on courses are now expected to import the benefits back into the school to help other staff. There is an emphasis on school-based INSET and drawing other partners into the school to support innovation.

Choice 8: Ethos

At the maintenance extreme, ethos is a mystery, something intangible and ineffable which a school simply possesses or lacks. At the development extreme, the most important aspect of ethos is the commitment to innovation and change. Staff who lack such enthusiasm are seen as damaging to the school's ethos. In the middle position, ethos is regarded as a product of the shared values and commitments of the school and its partners. Its most important aspect is the appreciation of staff and pupils. Ethos supports some development and change and can be improved by such activity.

We emphasize again the huge variety in the patterns of choices made by real schools. By no means are all schools to be fitted into the above sketches. The purpose of the sketches is to assist schools and officers to gain insight into what choices have been made and how they have contributed to the school's culture.

DEVELOPMENT AND MAINTENANCE EXTREMES

Schools whose overall profile is mixed or tends towards the middle recognize their existing strengths and see them as points for growth. At the same time, they acknowledge their limitations and so understand the potential power of development planning to guide and support innovation. Indeed, many such schools already engage in development planning, though they may not so call it or approach it in a systematic way.

Schools (or parts of schools) at the development extreme may be so confident in their innovative capacities that they take on too much too quickly. They will be good on plan construction, but much weaker on audit (since they will be reluctant to investigate weaknesses) and on evaluation (because the need to assess the effectiveness of implementation is seen as a distraction). They may also fail to see some of the more novel aspects of development planning, such as the need to involve the governing body.

There are at least two versions of schools (or parts of schools) at the maintenance extreme. The first is a school with a sound reputation and held in high regard by governors, parents and the local community. The head and staff are thus generally self-confident, anxious to maintain the status quo, and see little purpose in reform. Such schools do not necessarily have a capacity to cope with development and change.

The second version of the maintenance extreme is one which is seen as a 'poor' or 'failing' school. In many cases the head and (at least some) staff are defensive about the school, believing that the school's reputation is undeserved and blaming outside factors (government/LEA policy, lack of parental support, the quality of pupils, local conditions) for any perceived shortcomings. The school has a poor record of managing any innovation. There is a high level of anxiety and resistance shown toward any external innovation and a reluctance to accept direction, advice or support from the governing body or LEA officers.

Schools at the extremes of the profile need, at an early stage, to promote the conditions in which development can be seen in a positive light, properly managed and allowed to flourish. To put it another way, such a school needs to generate the conditions to support development planning if the school is to be genuinely improved. These conditions relate to the school's management arrangements, whereas the school's profile is a more general indication of its culture. The two are linked, the school's management arrangements being an aspect of its culture. In Chapter 3 we described the three dimensions of the management arrangements. Although the basic dimensions remain constant from school to school, the forms that they take reflect the choices the school makes about its culture.

USING THE DIAGNOSIS

The diagnosis of a school's culture can be used as a means of understanding, and perhaps anticipating, difficulties which the school might experience with development planning. In the larger school, the diagnosis may apply to part of the school, such as a subject department or faculty.

- *Example 1*. A school's approach to partners (Choice 2) and to support (Choice 7) may lead the school to undervalue the external assistance that can be drawn upon to help the school to manage a large amount of rapid change.

- *Example 2*. The existing organization of teaching and learning (Choice 4) may make it difficult to implement the National Curriculum which requires collaboration between teachers in different year groups and with different subject specialisms.

- *Example 3*. The choices can be seen to have influenced the school's management arrangements. One set of choices may have made it difficult for the school to have a framework of written policy statements. Another set of choices may have made it difficult to create 'horizontal' rather than 'vertical' teams which are needed to carry forward some kinds of development. Yet another set of choices may make it difficult for the school to provide opportunities for leadership to younger and more junior members of staff.

Through open discussion of the diagnosis of its culture, perhaps on a professional training day, a school can gain insight into how it should approach development planning. A good diagnosis allows a reasonable prognosis to be made. Consider the distinction, made in Chapter 6, between root and branch innovations. Some schools have such strong roots that they can successfully manage a wide range of branch innovations in a short time. In practice, most schools will need a mixture of root innovations and branch innovations and, through their development plan, will need to sequence them so that the appropriate root innovations precede the branch innovations which have to be adopted.

Schools with a more extreme profile (either maintenance or development) tend to lack roots on which to base the branch innovations now required. Yet they may well be tempted to take *only* branch innovations among their priorities. It is very unlikely that these can be implemented successfully; development planning is likely to be relatively unsuccessful; and the schools' capacity to cope with change is further weakened.

The innovations which these schools most need are root innovations but, unless there is a clear diagnosis at an early stage, they may not acknowledge this fundamental need and so be tempted to construct too ambitious a development plan with an inappropriate selection of priorities.

This conclusion affects these schools' approach to development planning and the guidance and support offered by the LEA. In the rest of this chapter we look at ways in which the diagnosis can help schools overcome difficulties at the various stages of development planning.

GETTING STARTED

Many schools pass through this preparatory stage quite quickly. For the schools under discussion, this stage may be dealt with far too quickly. As examples, there may be LEA (or governor) pressure to produce a development plan in a relatively short time and the head (of a school with an extreme maintenance profile) may interpret this demand as a task he or she must undertake personally and with reluctance. Or the head (of a school with an extreme development profile) may be fully convinced of the potential value of development planning, but have insufficient regard to the need to bring the rest of the staff to share this conviction.

In both cases there is insufficient understanding of and commitment to development planning to provide a reasonable chance of a successful outcome. 'Getting started' is in these schools the most critical stage, and yet it is in danger of being neglected. It is this stage which is likely to be slow and painful; it requires patience and the capacity to cope with indifference, rejection and hostility from those who remain unconvinced of the need for development planning and its benefits.

It will take skill and sensitivity from the head and/or LEA officers to establish a recognition of the groundwork that is necessary for successful development planning.

AUDIT

During this phase the schools need to identify and investigate the weaknesses in basic functioning. Part of the function of the audit stage is to create an explicit link between a school's strengths and weaknesses and external demands for change arising from national and LEA policies and initiatives. In the case of the schools under discussion, it is vital that the school comes to recognize its need for root innovations, especially those which improve the management arrangements, as part of the development plan. Sensitive and diplomatic assistance will be needed from officers if the school is to take this essential step. The head and other staff will probably assume that the existing management arrangements are perfectly satisfactory (as they may well have been for maintenance alone) and may feel threatened or insecure that these are now being questioned.

Examples are given below under:

- Frameworks.

- Changing roles.

- Working together.

Frameworks

None of the school's main policies may be available in a written form, because this seemed unnecessary as they were widely understood. Yet development planning usually involves some change to existing policies or the addition of new ones. Such changes easily create confusion in relation to existing policies. If existing policies are in a written form, it is easier to recognize what adjustments may be needed and then to communicate such modifications and the reason for them.

The school's approach to meetings may have been satisfactory in the past. Development planning establishes new teams, which need to meet. This can lead to an unanticipated 'meetings overload'. What is really required is a review of meetings to decide which existing meetings could be used to support development planning, which meetings could be abolished or reduced without detriment, how *all* meetings could be made more effective – all of this being a possible area for audit.

Clarifying Roles

Most people like to conduct their daily lives at work with a sense of security and order: regular routines make work comfortable and provide confidence. This is especially important for teachers, since life in classrooms is often unpredictable and exacting in its demands. Development planning requires teachers to accept new roles and responsibilities. The audit phase can be used as an opportunity for a senior member of staff to review the existing allocation of roles and responsibilities, both to see how satisfied everyone is with them and to check how they may need to be changed in development planning. An LEA officer may be able to detect problems here that are invisible to the head and staff.

The head and most senior staff may define management in a restricted way as their own role and responsibility. As we have seen in earlier chapters, development planning requires that *all* teachers become, and see themselves as, managers who share in the management of the school and its development. In the audit stage the head and senior staff (again perhaps with the help of an LEA officer or governor) may need to review their conceptions of management and their readiness to delegate management tasks to others, with trust and without feeling that they are losing status or security in their roles.

Working Together

The school may with justification believe that relationships between head and staff and between the teachers are good – warm, friendly and harmonious. Development planning, however, can introduce tension into such happy relationships because new forms of collaboration and teamwork may disturb the individual autonomy on which the harmony has rested. Every teacher knows that it is easy to be friendly with a colleague as long as one does not have to work with them. It is often the fear of upsetting these relationships that leads teachers to be apprehensive about the closer and intensive quality of relationships involved in collaboration and teamwork. The audit phase can be used to judge the quality and character of existing relationships and whether work is needed to prepare collaboration either among the staff or with the school's partners (see Resource File 7).

Most schools now have a staff development policy and a person or group to co-ordinate it. Development planning almost always requires some improvement to this policy, which is a key to providing the support staff need to give them the confidence and skill to meet the targets. The audit phase is a good time to review the staff development policy and how it may need to be adjusted to link more effectively to school development (see Resource File 8).

CONSTRUCTION

In schools with extreme profiles, great care needs to be taken in the selection of the priorities. Success is most likely when:

- the number of priorities chosen is very small;

- there are both root innovations and branch innovations;

- branch innovations are restricted as far as possible to those which cannot be postponed (e.g. National Curriculum);

- root innovations are selected to support the inescapable branch innovations, and special attention is given to root innovations that require changes to the management arrangements (e.g. those described in the section on audit above);

- short-term planning is determined in the light of longer-term goals.

In schools which are very poorly placed to engage in successful development planning, it may be helpful to introduce a review aspect to a root innovation chosen as a priority. That is, the action plan should have an element of review-type activity as well as innovation, since the time-scale for the development plan may allow too little time for an adequate audit in such a school. As it is demoralizing for a school to spend too long in the audit phase, review-type activities can be transferred to the action plan to provide a sound basis for planned change. Again, the school is likely to require skilful support to construct such a plan.

IMPLEMENTATION AND EVALUATION

In schools with an extreme profile, it is very important that the very first development plan is implemented with a degree of success. Such success breeds confidence and commitment and a readiness to embark on the second plan; failure breeds cynicism and a belief that time and energy have been expended to no purpose. Success in a school with an extreme maintenance profile convinces everyone that their initial reaction to development planning as an unnecessary intrusion was mistaken and that, contrary to expectation, the school has become a better place. Success in a school with an extreme development profile gives a sense of order and control over innovation, as well as greater consensus over the future direction of the school as a whole. The more thorough the evaluation of change, the more confidence there is that innovations can be consolidated within a maintenance system that gives the school stability.

In all schools some priorities are implemented with greater success than others. The head and LEA officers involved should make particular efforts to ensure the successful implementation of priorities that will serve as root innovations, since these establish permanent foundations for future development plans.

Diagnosing the difficulties in development planning is likely to be most effective when there is a strong partnership between schools and LEA officers. In this chapter we have considered this partnership mainly from the point of view of the school. We now change the focus to the LEA itself.

Chapter 12

Partnership between the LEA and Schools

This chapter describes the role of the LEA in development planning. The research was not able to show conclusively that some LEA approaches are more effective than others. Certain issues, however, arise in all LEAs and the chapter explains seven basic issues in the form of questions and tasks to which each LEA will choose its own response. The seven issues spring from what we have observed and from discussions with officers. They reflect what we rather tentatively believe to be good practice.

Although the chapter is primarily addressed to LEA officers (a term which includes advisers and inspectors), it could usefully be read by heads and teachers. If there is to be a successful partnership between schools and LEAs, governors, heads and staff need to have a thorough understanding of the role of the officers and the problems they currently face. Both this chapter and Resource File 4 are designed to promote such a partnership.

Most schools are at a relatively early stage in development planning and its management, and look to LEA officers to provide guidance and support. This is a considerable task for officers since they are, at the same time, having to respond to the Education Reform Act and, in particular, dealing with three urgent issues.

First, they are under pressure to provide support and guidance on a wide range of very specific innovations which schools need to implement according to a tight and relatively inflexible time-scale, e.g. the subjects of the National Curriculum and new modes of assessment, the introduction of the Local Management of Schools. This is stretching the education department and especially the advisory service which may find it difficult to meet the range and extent of demands being made upon it.

Secondly, at the same time, officers are working out their new relationships with elected members on the one hand and governing bodies and schools on the other.

Thirdly, an additional task is the construction of a strategy for monitoring and evaluation, often from the basis of an advisory service with little experience of inspectorial work. This may create problems both for the advisers and for headteachers, who are often unenthusiastic about the change towards inspectorial functions. A strategy for monitoring and evaluation will also involve changed relationships between education officers and advisers/inspectors.

The approach taken by the LEA to development planning is likely to be a major factor affecting the success of schools in development planning and its own success in responding to the Education Reform Act. The issues and questions listed below are designed to help officers to formulate or review the policy and strategy for development planning. Because of the considerable pressure upon them, many officers have had little opportunity to share ideas on development planning with other LEAs, have devised their policy and strategy very quickly to provide guidance for schools, and have had few opportunities to take stock.

ISSUE 1: THE DETERMINATION OF THE LEA POLICY TOWARDS DEVELOPMENT PLANNING

There are considerable variations between LEAs in the policies adopted towards development planning and development plans.

Among the important questions are:

- How was the LEA's policy determined? What consultation was involved and with whom?

- Has the LEA's policy been clearly communicated and justified? Does everyone involved understand the reason for particular policy decisions (e.g. whether development planning is obligatory or voluntary, the time-scale allowed for preparation/submission of development plans)? Who is responsible for the communication of the policy and for monitoring the effectiveness of the communication?

- Do the officers fully explain the benefits of development planning both for schools and for the LEA? Is the relation of the policy to other LEA policies clear to all?

- What commitment is there among the elected members, officers, governors, heads, teachers and parents to the LEA policy and how might the commitment be improved?

- Is the officers' role in development planning as clear as the policy?

Care taken by the LEA in preparing all those involved in school development planning is worth the effort. Officers need to be committed to the concept and may need in-service training if they are to be enabled to offer the support and advice they will undoubtedly be asked by schools to provide. Their roles and responsibilities need to be clear to avoid confusion among themselves or in their relationships with schools. They must have a clear grasp of the LEA's policy towards development planning and how this relates to the rest of their work with schools.

ISSUE 2: THE LEA'S CONCEPTION OF SCHOOL DEVELOPMENT PLANNING

There is a common confusion between *product* (school development plans as documents) and *process* (school development planning as activities). Officers often take the view that the latter is more important than the former. LEA documentation (e.g. guidelines), however, often gives the impression that they are more concerned with product than process.

There is also variation in the terminology adopted. Development plans, management plans, school plans, school development plans and institutional development plans are all in use and, so far as we can tell, mean much the same thing. When schools see different terms as meaning different or separate plans, there is a danger of confusion and discouragement. It is helpful if the officers clarify their own use of the various terms to ensure a degree of consistency within the LEA.

95

ISSUE 3: THE LEA'S DEVELOPMENT PLAN

Some LEAs have, and others are preparing, an LEA development plan. This is in part because they, like schools, are responding to innovations and changes which have to be planned and managed, and in part because an LEA development plan establishes a 'fit' between LEA policies and plans and those of schools, thus enhancing the partnership between officers and schools.

Among topics to be considered are:

- the construction and communication of the LEA development plan and the roles of members, officers and schools (governors, heads) in this task;

- the aims of the LEA development plan;

- the way in which the priorities of the LEA development plan are selected and turned into action plans;

- the relationship between the LEA's priorities, action plans and success criteria/performance indicators and those of the schools, and the extent to which they complement and support one another (see Figure 12.1).

ISSUE 4: INTEGRATION AND CO-ORDINATION OF DEVELOPMENT PLANS

When there is an LEA development plan, the task of integration and co-ordination of the work of the officers and of the schools is made much easier. Even when the LEA does not have a development plan, some attention to planning cycles will help schools with their development planning (see Resource File 5).

Questions to be considered are:

- How are the planning cycles of the LEA related to the planning cycles of the schools? Are schools expected to adapt their planning cycles to those of the LEA or has the LEA adjusted its own planning cycles where possible to help the schools?

- What is the impact of the above on the relationships between branches of the LEA, and their co-ordination with one another and with schools?

Some LEAs have phased in development plans over a period of time. This can help to resolve some of the early problems of co-ordination.

ISSUE 5: LEA USE OF DEVELOPMENT PLANS

LEAs frequently ask schools to submit their plans and/or documents linked with development plans and/or proformas provided by the LEA. This raises a number of questions:

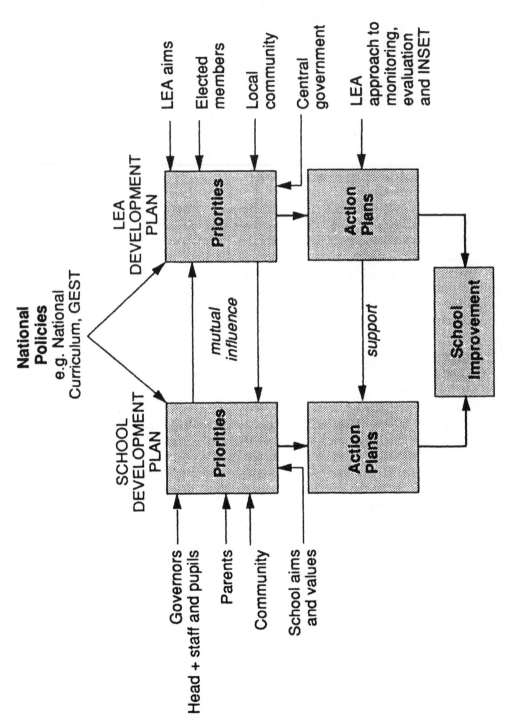

Figure 12.1 *School and LEA development plans*

- Does the LEA have good reasons for requiring schools to submit their plans in a particular form and at a particular time?

- Is it also clear to schools why this information is required, how it helps the LEA and/or the school, and how the information is used?

- Do the schools know that it has been used in the ways intended? Are they aware of the benefits of such use? What are the consequences if the plans are not used by the LEA as intended?

- Do officers provide 'feedback' to schools on their development plans?

- Does the LEA have a role in encouraging collaboration between schools in development planning?

Where LEAs require heads to submit the plan (whether or not in a prescribed format), it is helpful to make clear to schools what use they intend to make of them, for instance in relation to the identification of INSET needs and provisions. If LEAs intend to make judgements on the quality of the plans, heads will find it of practical value to be aware in advance of the criteria of such judgements. Schools usually like to know who will have access to the plans within the LEA. It has been shown to be helpful if an LEA officer makes a personal response to, and commentary upon, the submitted plan, and time needs to be allowed for this.

ISSUE 6: THE LEA SUPPORT SYSTEM FOR DEVELOPMENT PLANNING

Officers have much to contribute to successful school development planning in all its phases – getting started, audit, construction, implementation and evaluation – as indicated at various points in this book. In particular, they can contribute to the identification of strengths and weaknesses during the audit; to the selection of appropriate and realistic priorities and targets during plan construction; to the provision of in-service training and other forms of support during implementation; and to the evaluation of the implementation, an area in which many schools have little experience. There are a number of important topics involved here.

First, there is the form of the support provided:

- personal visits to schools by officers;
- guidelines;
- courses/INSET specifically directed to development planning;
- a 'permeation' approach in which issues in development planning form part of a wide range of INSET;
- advisory teachers with special expertise in development planning;
- courses provided by institutions for higher education.

As schools formulate their priorities and targets, they will identify INSET requirements to support implementation of the plan. For many schools this will lead to an improvement of INSET planning. Yet it may not be easy for LEAs to respond fully to the scale or variety of INSET sought by schools. It is helpful for schools to know as soon as possible how LEA provision of INSET is constrained, since this may influence the selection of development priorities. There should be a clear understanding between the LEA and heads of the means and time-scales for the effective co-ordination of INSET planning and provision. School development planning can enhance the identification of INSET needs, assist the LEA in the identification of local priorities, and improve the quality of the evaluation of the INSET provided.

Secondly, there is the difference in the kind of support needed by schools:

- when 'getting started';
- during the stages of development planning;
- after the first cycle.

Thirdly, there is the difference in the kind of support needed by:

- governors;
- heads and teaching staff;
- support staff.

Of the utmost importance is the preparation of heads and senior staff. Some LEAs have provided in-service support in the form of small conferences and workshops which bring together teams of two or three senior staff (always including the head, and if possible with the school's adviser/inspector) to discuss development planning, to examine any documentary advice and to engage in practical activities. The best in-service support seems to consist of a *series* of such meetings, with the option of on-site consultancy by an LEA officer between meetings. It is important to ensure that in all such meetings some heads with a known enthusiasm for school development planning be included. When the head and some senior staff have developed an understanding of and commitment to development planning, the task of preparing the rest of the staff is greatly facilitated and the sense of external pressure or imposition thereby reduced.

School development planning is relevant to the training provided for governors. LEAs should recognize the potential for confusion and conflict over the roles and responsibilities of governors, heads and teachers in relation to school development planning. This book gives more salience to governors than do many existing LEA guidelines because of the recent changes in their roles and responsibilities. The LEA may need to give advice and support to governors and heads in the light of their changing relationships.

ISSUE 7: THE RELATIONSHIP BETWEEN MONITORING AND EVALUATION AND DEVELOPMENT PLANNING

Development planning requires careful attention by schools to the ways in which they monitor and evaluate their own activities and the innovations they implement. LEAs have particular responsibilities for monitoring and evaluation following the Education Reform Act. In some cases, the LEA will need to add inspectorial functions to the work of the advisory service. In all LEAs there will be new forms of monitoring and evaluation, for example of financial delegation, which will involve education officers as well as advisers/inspectors.

In LEAs where there has been an advisory service with little or no inspectorial function, officers are likely to need training in the collection and interpretation of evidence about schools. When officers have a high level of skill in monitoring and evaluation, an important task for them is to train heads and teachers in these skills. This both helps schools to be more effective in development planning and makes monitoring and evaluation a shared responsibility between schools and LEA, which ensures 'quality assurance'.

Among the topics involved are:

- clarifying for schools the enhanced role of the LEA in monitoring and evaluation and the forms it will take;

- making adjustments in the roles, relationships and responsibilities of education officers and advisers/inspectors to exercise the functions of monitoring and evaluation;

- establishing an understanding of the relationship between the monitoring and evaluation carried out by officers (of all kinds) and the self-monitoring and self-evaluation activities conducted by schools themselves;

- discussing, clarifying and agreeing the criteria for evaluation and monitoring, on the basis of which judgements about success will be made both at the school and LEA level;

- clarifying, wherever possible, the basis of visits to schools by officers, whether to monitor/evaluate or to advise/support;

- ensuring that discussions during inspection visits are of the highest quality so that both the LEA and the school benefit from the experience;

- making certain that necessary information from inspection visits is systematically fed back to the advisory service in order to 'trigger' appropriate support;

- deciding the extent to which the LEA may use monitoring and evaluation data generated by schools as part of its own monitoring and evaluation activities, and the extent to which additional or independent monitoring and evaluation may be undertaken by officers;

- using all the data generated by the various forms of monitoring and evaluation both to support development planning by schools and to shape the LEA's own development plan.

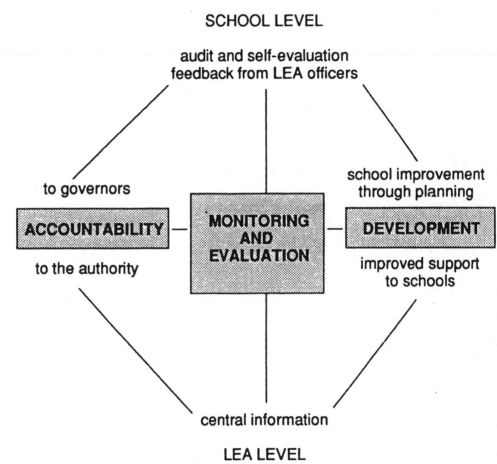

Figure 12.2 *The monitoring and evaluation diamond*

Development plans have enormous potential for contributing to the LEA's task of monitoring and evaluation. In effective development planning a considerable amount of self-evaluation by schools is involved in the processes of audit and evaluation. LEA officers can combine their task of monitoring with the school's own activities in a spirit of partnership, which both eases the LEA's task and enhances the skills of the staff in such monitoring and reporting. The development of performance indicators of various kinds can assist this partnership. (See Resource File 9 for a discussion of the relationship between performance indicators and success criteria in a development plan.) At the same time, LEA officers will recognize the tensions, at both LEA and school levels, between accountability and development. As Figure 12.2 indicates, improved monitoring at both levels can assist accountability *and* development. Schools may need support from LEA officers to understand fully how school development planning brings accountability and development into a mutually beneficial relationship. The figure illustrates how monitoring and evaluation relates to both accountability and development: the tasks are common to both schools and LEAs which have a complementary or mirror-image relationship in the process.

The way in which the LEA responds to these seven issues affects the quality of the partnership between the LEA and schools in development planning, the schools' perceptions of the LEA, and the capacity of schools to be successful in development planning and the management of innovation and change.

Chapter 13

Troubleshooting

Makers of modern technological appliances, such as computers and washing-machines, often provide in their instruction booklets a section on what to do when the machine breaks down or seems not to work – action that can be taken by oneself before giving up in despair or calling for outside help.

For some schools, development planning can be like this. The LEA guidelines or this book offered the instructions, which were read, but things have not turned out in the way they were supposed to. The trouble is that the school cannot return the guidance to the authors and ask for a new model or for its money back: the school appears to have failed in its work on development planning and there is little incentive to try again.

When things go wrong, what is to be done?

In this chapter we aim to provide some advice and support to heads and LEA officers who find themselves in this unenviable situation.

THE HEAD

The most difficult task for the head is to accept that he or she:

- must take some responsibility for the failure rather than blaming everybody else;

- cannot take all the blame because that becomes self-destructive;

- has the power to help everyone involved to interpret the failure as a positive learning experience.

The third element is perhaps the most important since it directs attention away from the very human tendency to apportion blame and to look for scapegoats. The head and senior staff, perhaps with an LEA officer or governor, need cool heads to analyse as openly and objectively as possible the factors that prevented success.

There are a number of questions that can be asked:

- *Did the head and senior staff really believe in the value of development planning?* If they did not, their lack of conviction and commitment will have been transmitted to the staff and undermined the process from the start. *Answer*: visit a school where development planning has been successful to see why they believe in it and the benefits they have derived.

  If they did believe in it, was it a belief not shared by the staff and all who were involved in the plan? *Answer*: let staff visit a school where development planning has worked – this will be more persuasive than argument.

- *Did the staff really understand the nature and process of development planning?* If not, then too little time was spent in preparation and in 'getting started'. *Answer:* conduct a post-mortem on the development plan that failed with the whole staff on a professional training day. Avoid absolutely the temptation to blame. Treat the occasion as an opportunity to learn about the process of development planning with a view to making it work at a second attempt. Build on the aspects that the school has done reasonably well, for not all aspects of the process will have been done badly.

- *Did the head and senior staff delegate real responsibility for management to the teachers?* If not, the staff will have had little ownership of the *process* of development planning, even though the plan itself was acceptable. In these circumstances the development plan has been seen by staff as the 'management's plan' – that is, a plan designed for and by 'the management' rather than for the benefit of the teachers and the school as a whole community. *Answer*: acknowledge this to the staff and explore how the head and senior staff can genuinely empower the teachers.

- *Were the existing management arrangements inappropriate to support development planning?* If so, this is far easier to recognize with hindsight. *Answer*: explore this hindsight with staff and use the occasion as an opportunity to review the management arrangements as a collective responsibility and a feature of the school which can be changed as part of the next development plan.

- *Was the plan too ambitious?* If so, the teachers will have suffered from innovation overload and taken on so much that everyone was very busy but very little seemed to be achieved. *Answer*: acknowledge the problem and explore how the size and scope of the next plan might be reduced to manageable proportions.

- *Did the school have a good plan but inadequate action plans?* If so, this is not surprising; indeed, this was one of the most common problems to emerge from our project and the reason why we have discussed the issue in depth in Chapter 7. *Answer*: recognize this is a widespread problem, maintain confidence in the work on plan construction, and focus attention on how well-designed action plans will help effective implementation of the next plan.

- *Did the head and senior staff assume that once the plan and the action plans were written they would run on automatic pilot?* If so, the difficulty may lie in insufficient care in sustaining commitment, checking progress and overcoming problems during implementation. *Answer*:

explore with staff how these aspects of implementation can be handled in the next plan.

These seven examples show that there are ways round initial difficulties or failure, if the head and senior staff accept a positive and constructive leadership role. It is vital, however, that these analytical discussions take place *within* the framework of development planning. Faced with failure, it is tempting for the head to conduct a post-mortem as an independent activity separated from the process of development planning. This is, of course, to treat development planning as readily separable from the school's 'normal' work and therefore as something which can be detached or rejected. This is in itself a misconception of development planning, which is in reality simply a different way of organizing what the school is already doing and what it needs to do. The analytical discussions must therefore be set within the process of development planning, as part of taking stock at the end of a cycle and of audit at the beginning of the next. To conduct the analysis in this way presumes a continuation of development planning and promotes discussion as an occasion for learning.

THE LEA OFFICER
When development planning fails, the officer will immediately recognize that it is the head who needs maximum support and encouragement. But there is much more to the officer's role, vital as this pastoral aspect is. There are various forms of practical assistance that may be required:

- Help with the management arrangements.
- As much protection as possible from pressures towards innovation.
- More LEA support than other schools.
- Developing a mutually agreed strategy.

These forms of assistance are discussed below.

Help with the Management Arrangements
The project has shown that the management arrangements play a key role in the success and failure of development planning. Many heads do not find it palatable when the arrangements have to be reviewed or questioned and rarely recognize that changes to them may be a valuable root innovation within the plan. The officer is in a good position to discuss the issue with the head in a non-threatening and supportive way or to suggest another head who may be better able to do so.

As Much Protection as Possible from Pressures towards Innovation
The limitation of the school's agenda to those branch innovations which are inescapable should greatly increase the school's chance of success, which is the essential condition of school improvement. This may mean that the school is not expected to give priority to the LEA's policies and innovations in the early years and that the

school should be discouraged from undertaking other forms of innovation outside the legal requirements.

More LEA Support than Other Schools

Such additional support may take various forms: extra time from inspectors/advisers: priority for consultancy support from the officers and for INSET opportunities; priority from LEA staff on professional training days to ensure that they are used effectively on the school's limited agenda for innovation; and additional resources, if possible, for specific deployment on the chosen agenda.

Developing a Mutually Agreed Strategy

To be successful, such support needs to be set within a strategy for the school designed in partnership between the officers and the school. The school may well have received support from the LEA in the past, but has failed to respond to it. This may be because, from the point of view of the school, the LEA approach seems to consist of tactics rather than a mutually agreed strategy. For instance, the school may have received considerable oral advice (which is ignored); opportunities for INSET for key individuals (which are not accepted or, if accepted, fail to feed back into the school as an impetus to institutional renewal); opportunities to visit other schools to observe good practice (which produces defensive rationales such as 'That won't work in our school because . . .').

A more strategic approach derives from a recognition that change is a relatively long-term process which cannot be done quickly or easily and that a carefully formulated step-by-step approach is to be preferred. This will require an alignment between the LEA's strategy for support and the school's slowly emerging strategy for its own development.

Strategic alignment of this kind is likely to involve:

- external support (of the kind described above);

- external pressure (without which the school may not move from its stable pattern of self-maintenance, e.g. an inspection, expressions of parental dissatisfaction);

- internal pressure (the recognition by the governors, head and senior staff of the advantages of development to the school itself);

- internal support (the release of self-help and self-directing energy which allows the school to break free from too great a dependence on LEA support).

Assistance of this kind from LEA officers enhances the partnership between the school and the LEA, and in particular between the head and the officer linked to the school. It also promotes 'self-managing schools' with reduced dependence on the LEA services, which is essential if these services are to escape being massively over-stretched. Most important of all, it is a partnership which can help more schools to be more successful in creating a better educated society.

PART FOUR

BROADER PERSPECTIVES

Chapter 14

School Effectiveness, School Improvement and Development Planning

We have sought to make this book a practical guide for schools who are managing change through development planning. To this end, we have attempted to avoid jargon, to write clearly, to express complex ideas simply and not to distract the reader with academic research and references. We are very much aware, however, that our work is but one example of a much broader concern by politicians, educators, parents and others in most Western countries with improving the quality of schooling.

Our work also fits into a current emphasis in educational research on the characteristics of effective schools and the strategies for school improvement. As much of this research is finding its way into educational policy and practice, we thought that it may be helpful in this chapter to extend our more practical treatment of development planning by taking a look at how it fits into this broader perspective. There are two reasons for doing this. First, the research we have chosen to refer to may be of some help to schools in their general approach to development planning. Secondly, much of this research is intrinsically interesting and may also provide a 'way into' a literature which at first glance may appear a little daunting (see also Resource File 10). The two areas of research that relate in particular to development planning are: the research on school effectiveness, the 'what'; and the research on school improvement, the 'how'. We discuss these in turn and in the final section of the chapter see how they relate to development planning.

SCHOOL EFFECTIVENESS

There is now a vast amount of evidence to support the common-sense notion that the characteristics of individual schools can make a difference to pupil progress. The research on 'effective schools', both in the UK (Mortimore et al., 1988) and the USA (Purkey and Smith, 1983), has found that certain internal conditions are typical in schools that achieve higher levels of outcomes for their students. The first major study conducted in the UK was by Rutter and his colleagues (1979) who compared the 'effectiveness' of ten secondary schools in Inner London on a range of student outcome measures. The 'effective schools', described in their book *Fifteen Thousand Hours*, were characterized by factors 'as varied as the degree of academic emphasis, teacher actions in lessons, the availability of incentives and rewards, good conditions for pupils, and the extent to which children are able to take responsibility' (Rutter et al., 1979, p. 178). It was this constellation of factors that Rutter and his colleagues later referred to as the school's 'ethos'. The HMI survey reported in *Ten Good Schools* comes to similar conclusions. To HMI the 'good school' is one that can demonstrate 'quality in its aims, in oversight of pupils, in curriculum design, in standards of teaching and academic achievements and in its links with the local community. What they all have in common is effective leadership and a "climate" that is conducive to growth' (DES, 1977, p. 36).

These descriptions of effective school cultures are similar to most others emerging from this line of research. The literature is also in agreement on three further issues. First, that these differences in outcome are systematically related to variations in the school's culture. Secondly, that the school's culture is amenable to alteration by concerted action on the part of the school staff. Although this is not an easy task, the evidence suggests that teachers and schools have more control than they may imagine over their ability to change their present situation. Thirdly, there is also broad agreement on the factors related to that difference.

In Boxes 14.1 and 14.2 we have selected extracts from two studies of school effectiveness. The first is from a widely quoted American review of the research literature. In this paper Purkey and Smith distinguish, helpfully in our opinion, between organizational and process factors related to effectiveness. The second extract is taken from the ILEA junior school study conducted by Mortimore and his colleagues. This extract contains a great deal of reference to teaching methods, which is a point that we will come back to when discussing our third extract.

Although this research is extremely helpful in gaining a greater degree of understanding of what makes for school effectiveness, there are however a number of problems with its practical applications. The first is to do with the tendency of educational administrators, in their search for simple solutions to complex problems, naively to regard research evidence as a panacea for their pressing educational concerns. For as Cuban (1983) points out, too narrow an interpretation of the school effectiveness criteria leads to an increase in standardization, a narrowing of the educational agenda, and a removal of the obligation to improve from schools that have good examination results. Cuban argues that the question should really be: 'How can the broader more complex and less easily measured goals of schooling be achieved *as* we improve test scores?' In this respect, the effectiveness criteria have too narrow a focus for a practical strategy.

The second problem is raised by the increased sophistication of the recent school effectiveness studies. New analytical techniques have enabled more detailed investigation of the differential impact of school effectiveness on sub-groups. Mortimore and his colleagues (1988), for example, found that there was some variability in progress in reading between boys and girls in the same junior schools. Nuttall and his colleagues (1989), in their study of ILEA secondary schools, found that the effectiveness of a school varies along several dimensions, and that there are also variations over time. These findings suggest that the school effectiveness criteria lack the comprehensiveness required for a practical whole-school strategy.

We were recently reminded of a third problem when reviewing a book of school effectiveness case studies from the USA (Taylor, 1990). Although there was clarity and consensus in the cases about the effective school correlates, there was little discussion about the nature of the *process* that leads to effectiveness. Nowhere in the cases was the process of translating the correlates into a programme of action sufficiently articulated. And this of course is the third problem.

Even from this brief review, it is clear that there is a great deal of similarity between the characteristics of the 'effective school' and our description of the management arrangements appropriate for sustaining school development planning. It is also

Box 14.1 *Effective schools: organization and process factors*

The following eight factors are representative of the so-called 'organization factors' that are characteristic of effective schools (see Purkey and Smith, 1983):

1 Curriculum-focused school leadership.

2 Supportive climate within the school.

3 Emphasis on curriculum and teaching (for example, maximizing academic learning).

4 Clear goals and high expectations for students.

5 A system for monitoring performance and achievement.

6 On-going staff development and in-service training.

7 Parental involvement and support.

8 LEA and external support.

These factors do not, however, address the dynamics of schools as organizations. There appear to be four additional factors which infuse some meaning and life into the process of improvement within the school. These 'process factors' provide the means of achieving the organizational factors; they lubricate the system and 'fuel the dynamics of interaction'. They have been described by Fullan (1985, p. 400) as follows:

1 A feel for the process of leadership; this is difficult to characterize because the complexity of factors involved tends to deny rational planning – a useful analogy would be that organizations are to be sailed rather than driven.

2 A guiding value system; this refers to a consensus on high expectations, explicit goals, clear rules, a genuine caring about individuals, etc.

3 Intense interaction and communication; this refers to simultaneous support and pressure at both horizontal and vertical levels within the school.

4 Collaborative planning and implementation; this needs to occur both within the school and externally, particularly in the LEA.

Box 14.2 *The twelve key factors of junior school effectiveness*
Adapted from Mortimore *et al.* (1988), pp. 250–6

1 **Purposeful leadership of the staff by the head**
   Key aspects: effective heads are sufficiently involved in and
   knowledgeable about what goes on in classrooms and about progress of
   individual pupils. Although they do not interfere constantly they are not
   afraid to assert their leadership.

2 **The involvement of the deputy head**
   Key aspects: a certain amount of delegation by the head and the sharing
   of responsibilities promote effectiveness.

3 **The involvement of teachers**
   Key aspects: active involvement in curriculum planning, developing
   curriculum guidelines, and participation in decision-making on school
   policy.

4 **Consistency among teachers**
   Key aspects: continuity in teaching staff and consistency of teacher
   approach are important.

5 **Structured sessions**
   Key aspects: teachers organize a framework within which pupils can
   work, encourage a degree of independence, and allow some freedom
   within this structure.

6 **Intellectually challenging teaching**
   Key aspects: use of higher-order questions and statements, pupils
   encouraged to use their creative imagination and powers of problem
   solving, teachers have an enthusiastic approach, and high expectations
   of pupils.

Box 14.2 *The twelve key factors of junior school effectiveness* (continued)
Adapted from Mortimore *et al.* (1988), pp. 250–6

---

7 **Work-centred environment**
Key aspects: much content-related work and feedback, relatively little time spent on routine matters, a low level of noise, and not an excessive amount of pupil movement.

8 **Limited focus within lessons**
Key aspects: a focus upon only one curriculum area during a lesson.

9 **Maximum communication between teachers and pupils**
Key aspects: a flexible approach, blending individual, class and group interaction as appropriate, including class discussion.

10 **Record keeping**
Key aspects: record keeping linked to planning and assessment by both head and teachers.

11 **Parental involvement**
Key aspects: help in classrooms, on educational visits, attendance at meetings to discuss children's progress, parents' reading to their children and access to books at home, informal open door policy rather than parent–teacher associations.

12 **Positive climate**
Key aspects: more emphasis on praise and reward than punishment and control, enthusiastic attitude of teachers, involvement of staff and children in a range of activities outside the classroom.

Box 14.3 *The findings of the research on teaching effects*
Adapted from Doyle (1987), pp. 93–6

A summary of the substantive findings from studies of teaching effects falls into three broad categories:

1 **Time and curriculum**. Student achievement is influenced by the way time is allocated by teachers and used by students in classrooms. It follows that interventions which affect instructional time are likely to affect achievement. But time alone is not the measure of quality in teaching. At the very least, our conception of time in classrooms must include a dimension of curriculum. Curriculum most often shows up in studies of teaching as content covered and/or opportunity to learn. The most sophisticated form of this measure is 'academic learning time', i.e. the time students spend working successfully with content measured on the criterion achievement test. In thinking about instructional time it is necessary to consider not only whether students are paying attention, but also what they are doing: solving work problems, answering comprehension questions, writing expository essays – and whether these 'pursuits' are related to the curriculum being tested. When alignment occurs, students achieve. In this sense opportunity to learn is a fundamental condition for student achievement.

2 **Classroom management**. Whether students actually utilize their opportunities to learn depends in part upon how well teachers organize and manage classrooms. Central to this view of classroom order is a *work system* consisting of activities which organize students for working and rules and procedures which specify actions for routine events. The most important feature of the work system for a class are the *programmes of action* that define the nature of order for particular segments of time and pull students along specified paths. The teachers' role in management has at least three dimensions. First, they prepare in advance for how students as a group will be organized to accomplish work and what rules and procedures will govern movement and routine events. Secondly, successful teachers communicate their work systems clearly to students through explanations, written materials, rehearsals and sanction. Thirdly, successful teachers monitor classroom events to make sure that the work system is operating within reasonable limits and to notice early signs of potential disruptions.

Box 14.3 *The findings of the research on teaching effects* (continued)
Adapted from Doyle (1987), pp. 93–6

3 **Dimensions of instructional quality**. Given equal emphases on content and equally orderly classrooms, differences in student achievement will result among classes from differences in the quality of instruction, that is, the design of assignments, the clarity of explanations, the chances students have to practise, and the availability and accuracy of feedback. A complete picture of effective teaching must include, therefore, dimensions of instructional quality.

Classroom studies of teaching effects have generally supported a direct and structured approach to instruction. That is, students usually achieve more when a teacher:

a emphasizes academic goals, makes them explicit and expects students to be able to master the curriculum;
b carefully organizes and sequences curriculum experiences;
c clearly explains and illustrates what students are to learn;
d frequently asks direct and specific questions to monitor students' progress and check their understanding;
e provides students with ample opportunity to practise, gives prompts and feedback to ensure success and correct mistakes, and allows students to practise a skill until it is overlearned or automatic;
f reviews regularly and holds students accountable for work.

From this perspective, a teacher promotes student learning by being active in planning and organizing instruction, explaining to students what they are to learn, arranging occasions for guided practice, monitoring progress, providing feedback, and otherwise helping students to understand and accomplish work.

clear that the effective school's criteria provide a necessary but not sufficient condition for school development. These characteristics can, however, be used in an audit or review much in the same way as we suggested a review of the school's management arrangements in Chapter 3. For example: What can your school learn from them? How can aspects of them be incorporated into your development plan?

The research on school effectiveness is relatively recent and has been preceded by an extensive body of research on the effects of teaching on student performance. A summary of the research on teaching effects is given in Box 14.3. This research, much of it from the USA, generally follows a 'process–product' design, where the amount and quality of teaching is assessed and correlated with student test scores. Within this framework the researchers attempt to identify those patterns of teaching that relate to enhanced achievement: the focus is on teaching as a means to an end. Although researchers in this area speak confidently to their conclusions, we must remember that at best their results are correlations, and do not prove 'cause and effect'. The health warnings that we gave to the research on school effects apply here also.

We discuss this research for two reasons. The first is that, as the Mortimore study on school effects shows, teaching is an important aspect of school effectiveness. Indeed some researchers claim that the major contributor to school effectiveness is teaching rather than school culture. Be that as it may, we do know that the more structured and reflective the approach to teaching, the more likely it is that students' academic performance will improve. These specifications can therefore be used by teachers as a basis for auditing and reviewing their own teaching.

The second and related reason is that teacher development and school development are inextricably linked. As we argued in Chapter 3, management is everyone's responsibility and the school's development plan provides a structure for integrating classroom and whole-school developments. On the one hand, classroom improvement is about enhancing teaching skills and strategies, curriculum development and classroom management. On the other hand, school development is about improving the school's management arrangements, the structures, roles and collaboration necessary for sustained improvement. In the middle, linking the two, is the teacher. It is only he or she who can bring together in a practical and meaningful way these two crucial elements for enhancing quality in schools.

We believe that some of the research quoted and alluded to above may help teachers become more precise in their search for increased effectiveness. But we must remember that research in general has, as we have noted, many limitations. In terms of school development it becomes useful only when it is subjected to the discipline of practice, through the exercise of the teacher's professional judgement. For as Stenhouse (1975, p. 142) said in a slightly different context, such proposals are not to be regarded 'as an unqualified recommendation but rather as a provisional specification claiming no more than to be worth putting to the test of practice. Such proposals claim to be intelligent rather than correct.'

The research discussed in this section is limited in one other respect: it has been more concerned to describe the characteristics of school effectiveness, rather than suggest ways in which effectiveness can be achieved. In the following section we examine some other research which is more concerned with the process of improving schools.

SCHOOL IMPROVEMENT

School improvement studies tend to be more action-oriented than the effective schools research. They embody the long-term goal of moving towards the vision of the 'problem solving' or 'thinking' school. This attitude was exemplified in the work of the OECD-sponsored International School Improvement Project (ISIP) and the knowledge that emanated from it. School improvement was defined in the ISIP as (Van Velzen *et al.*, 1985, p. 48):

> a systematic, sustained effort aimed at change in learning conditions and other related internal conditions in one or more schools, with the ultimate aim of accomplishing educational goals more effectively.

School improvement is therefore about developing strategies for educational change that strengthen the school's organization, as well as implementing curriculum reforms. This obviously implies a very different way of thinking about change than the ubiquitous 'top-down' approach so popular with policy-makers. When the school is regarded as the 'centre' of change, then strategies for change need to take this new perspective into account. The ISIP served to popularize a school improvement approach to educational change, and we have summarized so-called ISIP knowledge in Box 14.4.

The ISIP approach to change is highly consistent with the message of this book. We too envisage the school at the centre of change, endorse the emphasis on curriculum priorities being linked to managerial change within the plan, and would like to see the school operating within a supportive environment.

We also are concerned about the long-term impact of change. As we noted in Chapter 2, all too often change efforts are short-lived; they either do not survive early enthusiasm or are replaced too quickly by another 'fad' or 'good idea'. The ISIP approach emphasized that effective change is a long-term process and a complex one at that. This complexity has been the subject of a number of investigations over the past ten years or so. Happily we now have a much better idea of what the change process looks like, and what are the factors making for success. We have summarized in Box 14.5 the main stages of the school improvement process as it applies to school development planning.

We are pleased to report that other school improvement research is consistent with our general advice. This research is generally of two types. The first are the reviews of research that attempt to distil general guidelines from a synthesis of a number of studies. The second are the individual, usually in-depth, studies of school improvement.

An example of the first type is Fullan's (1991) *The New Meaning of Educational Change*. The book contains a comprehensive review of current research on educational change and practice. From this synthesis, Fullan identifies a number of assumptions about change which are important determinants of whether the realities of change get confronted or ignored. These assumptions about change are given in Box 14.6.

An example of the second type of research is Louis and Miles' (1990) study, *Improving the Urban High School*. The book describes in depth school improvement efforts in five large American urban high schools. In contrast to studies of effective

117

Box 14.4 *A summary of ISIP knowledge*
Adapted from Van Velzen (1985) and Hopkins (1987)

The approach to school improvement taken by the ISIP rests on a number of assumptions:

1 **The school as the centre of change**. This means that external reforms need to be sensitive to the situation in individual schools, rather than assuming that all schools are the same. It also implies that school improvement efforts need to adopt a 'classroom-exceeding' perspective, without ignoring the classroom.

2 **A systematic approach to change**. School improvement is a carefully planned and managed process that takes place over a period of several years.

3 **A key focus for change** is the 'internal conditions' of schools. These include not only the teaching–learning activities used in the school, but also the school's procedures, role allocation and resource use that support the teaching–learning process (in our words the school's management arrangements).

4 **Accomplishing educational goals more effectively**. Generally speaking, educational goals are what a school is *supposed* to be doing for its students and society. This suggests a broader definition of outcome than student scores on achievement tests, even though for some schools these may be pre-eminent. Schools also serve the more general developmental needs of students, the professional development of teachers and the needs of its community.

5 **A multi-level perspective**. Although the school is the centre of change it does not act alone. The school is embedded in an educational system that has to work collaboratively or symbiotically if the highest degrees of quality are to be achieved. This means that the roles of teachers, heads, governors, parents, support people (advisers, higher education, consultants, etc.), and local authorities should be defined, harnessed and committed to the process of school improvement.

6 **Integrative implementation strategies**. This implies a linkage between 'top-down' and 'bottom-up' – remembering of course that both approaches can apply at a number of different levels in the system. Ideally 'top-down' provides policy aims, an overall strategy and operational plans; this is complemented by a 'bottom-up' response involving diagnosis, priority goal setting and implementation. The former provides the framework, resources and a menu of alternatives; the latter, energy and school-based implementation.

7 **The drive towards institutionalization**. Change is only successful when it has become part of the natural behaviour of all those in the school. Implementation by itself is not enough.

Box 14.5 *The process of school improvement and development planning*
After Miles (1986)

In most schools development planning will initially be an innovation, a change from current practice. Even though development planning is supposed to help schools manage innovation and change, it may, particularly at the outset, represent a considerable challenge. For this reason it is helpful to regard the introduction of development planning as an innovation problem in itself, and to draw on the knowledge that we have of the change process.

The innovation process is generally considered to consist of three overlapping phases:

1 **Initiation**. This phase is about deciding to embark on development planning, and about developing commitment towards the process. During this phase the purposes and process of development planning should be clearly spelled out, a key person in the school should be prepared to argue the case and encourage others to participate, and the focus of the whole process should be linked to issues that are important to a majority in the school. During this phase pressure to be involved is acceptable, as long as it is accompanied by support.

2 **Implementation**. This phase normally includes the first cycle of development planning when the school is learning how to carry out the process. During this phase development planning needs to be well co-ordinated, have adequate and sustained INSET support, and 'rewards' (in the form of supply cover, positive reinforcement, etc.) should be provided. It is during this phase that skills and understanding are being acquired, some success is being achieved and responsibility is delegated to working groups of teachers.

3 **Institutionalization**. This phase occurs when development planning becomes part of the school's usual pattern of doing things. Management arrangements of the type described in Chapter 3 have evolved to support both development and maintenance, and are part of everyone's usual pattern of behaviour. There is widespread use of action plans by staff, the impact of development planning is being seen on classroom practice, and the whole process is not now regarded as being unusual.

The failure of many change efforts to progress beyond early implementation is partially explained by the lack of realization on the part of those involved that each of these phases has different characteristics and requires different strategies if success is to be achieved.

Box 14.6 *Assumptions about change*
Source: Fullan (1991), pp. 105–7

1 Do not assume that your version of what the change should be is the one that should or could be implemented. On the contrary, assume that one of the main purposes of the process of implementation is to *exchange your reality* of what should be through interaction with others.

2 Assume that any significant innovation, if it is to result in change, requires individuals to work out their own meaning. Significant change involves a certain amount of ambiguity, ambivalence and uncertainty for the individual about the meaning of change.

3 Assume that conflict and disagreement are not only inevitable but fundamental to successful change. Since any group of people possess multiple realities, any collective change attempt will necessarily involve conflict.

4 Assume that people need pressure to change (even in directions which they desire), but it will only be effective under conditions which allow them to react, to form their own position, to interact with others and to obtain support.

5 Assume that effective change takes time. It is a process of 'development in use'. Unrealistic or undefined time-lines fail to recognize that implementation occurs developmentally. Persistence is a critical attribute of successful change.

6 Do not assume that the reason for lack of implementation is outright rejection of the values embodied in the change or hard-core resistance to all change. Assume that there are a number of possible reasons.

7 Do not expect all or even most people or groups to change. The complexity of change is such that it is totally impossible to bring about widespread reform in any large social system. Progress occurs when we take steps which *increase* the number of people affected.

8 Assume that you will need a *plan* which is based on the above assumptions and which addresses the factors known to affect implementation. Evolutionary planning and problem-coping models based on knowledge of the change process are essential.

9 Assume that no amount of knowledge will ever make it totally clear what action should be taken. Better knowledge of the change process will improve the mix of resources on which we draw, but it will never and should never represent the sole basis for decision.

10 Assume that changing the culture of institutions is the real agenda, not implementing single innovations. Putting it another way: when implementing particular innovations, always pay attention to how the institution is developing or not.

schools and effective teaching, they set themselves the task of answering the question, 'How do we get there?' They had five major findings on what it takes to really improve 'big-city' schools.

Their first is to do with *school–LEA relationships*. They found that this worked best when the LEA provided support and direction, and the school had a great deal of autonomy in choosing goals and strategies. Effective working relationships were the key.

A second factor specifically relates to the theme of this book. Louis and Miles found that an *evolutionary approach to planning* 'works best, with plenty of early action (small-scale wins) to create energy and support learning'. They also claim that 'planning is the first point where empowerment takes hold' (p. 292).

The third factor which also resonates with themes in this book is the importance of *shared images* 'of what the school should become' (p. 293). The importance of generating ownership towards the school's vision and aims and their reflection in the priorities of the plan is crucial.

Fourthly, Louis and Miles mention *resources* as a key variable. They call 'for a broad based view of resources' in support of the school's vision. They emphasize the linking of developmental priorities to a cool appraisal of the resource implications.

Finally, Louis and Miles refer to *problem coping*. They found that, 'problems during school improvement efforts are multiple, pervasive, and often nearly intractable. But dealing with them actively, promptly, and with some depth is the single biggest determinant of program success' (p. 295). 'Depth', they emphasize, is not about 'fire-fighting' but, to use our language, is about dealing directly with the school's management arrangements.

So there is a considerable body of research-based knowledge that can help with designing development planning initiatives, whether at the LEA, school or staff working group level. Once again we need to issue the familiar health warning. Not all of this advice need apply to every school, but much of it is by now well enough tested to warrant serious consideration.

So far the discussion has been on general strategic approaches to change. There is, however, one other area of school improvement research that needs mentioning briefly. This is the collection of specific individual approaches, that one commentator has recently referred to as being 'doors' which can open or unlock the process of school improvement (Joyce, 1991).

There are a number of familiar 'doors' that we have passed through during the recent history of educational change in the UK. A much-opened door in the early 1980s was the one named school self-evaluation. There were first the LEA-initiated schemes which tended to be accountability- rather than development-oriented (see Clift *et al.*, 1987). Later, the GRIDS approach sponsored by the Schools Council offered schools a more autonomous and developmental approach to whole-school evaluation which became very popular (see Abbott *et al.*, 1988). Other 'doors' have been the 'discovery' of management training in 1983, changes in INSET funding in the mid 1980s, and categorically funded curriculum projects such as TVEI.

The American research on these individual strategies has been more focused than their British counterparts. The tradition in the USA, as we have already seen, is to relate specific strategies to student test scores as a measure of effectiveness. Using this approach, in inevitably limited situations, some school improvement strategies have produced startling results. For example, the research on the application of different 'Models of Teaching', as described by Joyce and Weil (1986), has resulted in consistently higher test scores in some classrooms. Co-operative learning is currently achieving consistent improvements in many classrooms across the USA. The direct use of technology in classrooms, e.g. television programmes such as 'Sesame Street', and collaborative approaches to staff development, e.g. coaching, have well-documented positive effects on student learning (Joyce and Showers, 1988).

Unfortunately not all school improvement strategies work well all the time and in every setting. When they do not it is often because they do not affect the culture of the school. Many of these strategies implicitly assume that behind the 'door' are a series of interconnecting pathways that lead inexorably to school improvement. This is not so. Too often they focus on individual changes, on discrete projects and on individual teachers and classrooms, rather than on how these changes can fit in with and adapt the organization and culture of the school. As a consequence when the door opens it leads only into a cul-de-sac.

In addressing the same issue, Fullan (1988, p. 29) commented that:

> Without a direct and primary focus on changes in organizational factors it is unlikely that [single innovations or specific projects] will have much of a reform impact, and whatever impact there is will be short lived . . . school improvement efforts which ignore these deeper organizational conditions are 'doomed to tinkering' . . . Strategies are needed that more directly address the culture of the organization.

To conclude this section, let us restate the main problem with most attempts at school improvement. They are successful only to the extent that they satisfactorily address the complexities of school culture. This is something that, as we have argued in Chapter 3, development planning as a school improvement strategy is well able to do. We return to this crucial issue in the final section.

SCHOOL DEVELOPMENT

It is now over ten years since Ron Edmonds asked his felicitous question: 'How many effective schools would you have to see to be persuaded of the educability of all children?' He continued, 'We already know more than we need to do that. Whether or not we do it must depend on how we feel about the fact that we haven't so far.'

Although we now know a lot more about school effectiveness and improvement than when Edmonds wrote, student achievement still lags far behind society's expectations. It seems to us that one of the major difficulties is the way in which this knowledge is used. Knowledge of the type discussed in this chapter is not a panacea; at best it is informed advice that schools may wish to test out in their own settings. Our advice on development planning must be seen in the same light. The advantage of development planning, however, is that it provides a means whereby this knowledge can be put to the test of practice. The knowledge is there to inform, not control practice. To return to Edmonds' question, it is an implicit argument of this book that when research-based knowledge is put to the test of practice, the result will be more schools which educate *all* of their pupils.

For this to be achieved requires not simply better research, however practitioner friendly, but a profound change in school culture. Although few schools have yet achieved this cultural change, many are working on it. Where a school lacks the appropriate culture, development planning is a means of achieving it. The recognition by schools of this fact is the real and important condition of development planning. This is the key insight. If the school does so recognize, it will understand that development planning is not just about implementing innovation and change, but about changing its culture – or in more concrete terms, its management arrangements – to improve its *capacity* to manage (other) changes. A school cannot fend off change until it has recreated its culture. But it can self-consciously make changes to its management arrangements through its development plan, so that the *process* of development planning is strengthened simultaneously with implementing other kinds of innovations.

The main purpose of our writing in this way has *not* been to contribute to the academic literature on school effectiveness, school improvement or management. Rather it has been to persuade heads and teachers that thinking about themselves, their work and their school in certain ways is empowering. It can help transform the culture of the school, and make it a better and more effective place for all pupils and teachers to learn.

REFERENCES

Abbott, R. *et al.* (1988) *GRIDS School Handbooks*, 2nd edition, Primary and Secondary versions. York: Longman for the SCDC.

Clift, P. *et al.* (1987) *Studies in School Self-Evaluation*. Lewes: Falmer Press.

Cuban, L. (1983) 'Effective schools: a friendly but cautionary note', *Phi Delta Kappan*, **64** (10) (June), 695–6.

DES (1977) *Ten Good Schools*. London: HMSO.

Doyle, W. (1987) 'Research on teaching effects as a resource for improving instruction', in Wideen, M. and Andrews, I. (eds) *Staff Development for School Improvement*. Lewes: Falmer Press.

Fullan, M. (1985) 'Change processes and strategies at the local level', *The Elementary School Journal*, **85** (3), 391–421.

Fullan, M. (1988) 'Change processes in secondary schools: towards a more fundamental agenda'. University of Toronto (mimeo).

Fullan, M. (1991) *The New Meaning of Educational Change*. London: Cassell.

Hopkins, D. (ed.) (1987) *Improving the Quality of Schooling*. Lewes: Falmer Press.

Joyce, B. (1991) 'The doors to school improvement', *Educational Leadership* (May), 59–62.

Joyce, B. and Showers, B. (1988) *Student Achievement through Staff Development*. New York: Longman.

Joyce, B. and Weil, M. (1986) *Models of Teaching*, 3rd edition. Englewood Cliffs, NJ: Prentice-Hall.

Louis, K. S. and Miles, M. (1990) *Improving the Urban High School*. New York: Teachers College Press.

Miles, M. (1986) 'Research findings on the stages of school improvement'. New York: Centre for Policy Research (mimeo).

Mortimore, P. *et al.* (1988) *School Matters*. London: Open Books.

Nuttall, D. *et al.* (1989) 'Differential school effectiveness', *International Journal of Educational Research*, **13** (10), 769–76.

Purkey, S. and Smith, M. (1983) 'Effective schools: a review', *The Elementary School Journal*, **83** (4), 427–52.

Rutter, M. *et al.* (1979) *Fifteen Thousand Hours*. London: Open Books.

Stenhouse, L. (1975) *An Introduction to Curriculum Research and Development*. London: Heinemann Educational Books.

Taylor, B. (ed.) (1990) *Case Studies in Effective Schools Research*. Dubuque, IA: Kendall/Hunt Publishing Company for the Center for Effective Schools.

Van Velzen, W. *et al.* (1985) *Making School Improvement Work*. Leuven, Belgium: ACCO.

PART FIVE

RESOURCE FILE

The contents of this resource file are intended to guide those seeking further information about particular issues raised in the book, as follows:

1 Turning aims and goals into policy statements.

2 Devising strategies for managing development and change.

3 Making meetings effective.

4 Integrating school and LEA monitoring and evaluation systems.

5 Co-ordinating school and LEA planning cycles.

6 Working out relationships between governors, head and staff.

7 Collaboration and teamwork.

8 Devising a staff development policy linking individual to institutional development.

9 Success criteria and performance indicators.

10 Annotated bibliography.

Resource File 1:

Turning Aims and Goals into Policy Statements

In *The Self-Managing School* (Lewes: Falmer Press, 1988) Brian Caldwell and Jim Spinks define a policy as a set of guidelines which provide a framework for achieving a purpose or goal. A policy specifies in general terms the kind of action to be taken in relation to an issue, with the rules or procedures for implementing the policy.

At the present time, for example, many schools are preparing a written policy on assessment. It lists the purposes or functions of assessment (including marking and recording) and then the actions to be undertaken by teachers to put the policy into effect.

Written policies:

- provide an explicit link between aims (goals) and action;

- give unambiguous guides for action, ensuring consistency between teachers in operating the policy;

- save time and help to avoid confusion or conflict;

- allow the school to check consistency between policies;

- ease the induction of new staff;

- help the school to explain to its partners what it is doing and why;

- support planning, since sound policies are part of the maintenance system, and poor policies or lack of policy become a priority for development;

- should not exceed one side of A4 in length.

If an issue is uncontentious, making a written policy is an easy task, the documentation of existing practice. If the issue is contentious, creating the policy will need much more time and care.

Devising Strategies for Managing Development and Change

A *strategy* provides the framework for solving problems in development planning, and includes:

- a definition of the purpose or goal to be reached;

- an outline of the main pathways for reaching the goal;

- a planned time frame for reaching the goal;

- an estimate of the costs (time, money, personnel and other resources) needed to reach the goal.

Tactics are the detailed operational activities required to put the strategy into effect. A strategy can be implemented by a variety of tactics, the choice being constrained by the circumstances of the time and location. Tactics are sometimes changed in the light of experience or prevailing conditions and constraints.

Keeping in mind the distinction between strategy and tactics can help effective development planning in the following ways:

- Do not get distracted by, or bogged down in, tactical details until the strategy is clear – to do so makes decision making more difficult.

- Do not abandon a strategy just because a particular tactic will not work or fails – choose another tactic.

- Remember that tactical variation makes strategies more flexible and adaptable than they seem.

- Remember that tactics are opportunities for those involved to use their creativity and inventiveness whilst implementing the strategy.

Resource File 3:

Making Meetings Effective

Meetings are usually considered to be formal occasions where a group of people discuss business prepared on the basis of an agenda, often with supporting papers. A short discussion between two or three teachers over coffee at break is also a form of meeting. Development planning involves meetings of all kinds, and they all use that precious commodity – time. The following are guides to the efficient use of meetings:

- Keep *formal* meetings to a minimum: use the informal kind unless there is a good reason for greater formality.

- Make sure that a meeting has, from the beginning, very clear terms of reference to keep discussion to the point.

- Make the membership as small as possible for the meeting to discharge its responsibilities: the larger the meeting the more difficult it is to fix times when all will be present.

- Choose the right people to be members – those who can best contribute to the task, rather than those who need to know about the outcomes of the meeting, which is a matter for communication.

- Fix limits to the meeting and decide a finishing time beforehand or at the start of the meeting. This concentrates the mind on the business, inhibits diversions and prevents the meeting dissolving by early departures.

- Choose the person who can chair the meeting most effectively. This may not be a member with the most seniority or status.

- Where minutes need to be kept, decide what needs to be recorded and reported and make sure the minutes are short and clear. Use an 'action column' to record who is going to do what before the next meeting.

- Provide copies of these brief minutes only to those who need to know or who are known to be interested. If unsure, ask who wants the minutes rather than sending them to everyone.

- Avoid setting meeting times which conflict with other commitments of members.

- Choose a location and furniture arrangement appropriate to the kind of meeting required.

- When a meeting has to report to a larger meeting, plan carefully to fit into the cycle.

Resource File 4:

Integrating School and LEA Monitoring and Evaluation Systems

Development planning requires schools to monitor and evaluate themselves in explicit ways – in the audit and during, as well as at the end of, the implementation of a priority. LEAs already have schemes by which advisers/inspectors monitor and evaluate schools by reviews and inspections; many LEAs are developing new approaches to such work.

Monitoring and evaluation is most effective when there is a partnership between schools and LEA officers, and the two approaches are integrated to create the maximum mutual benefit. Some of the ways in which this can be achieved are as follows:

- Reviews or inspections by LEA officers are arranged to fit in with the cycle of development planning, so that they contribute at the most appropriate stages.
- The school recognizes that the audit, the 'progress checks' and the 'success checks' are powerful sources of self-monitoring and self-evaluation data.
- The school makes use of data generated by officers to help identify future needs and priorities in the development plan; and officers use data generated by the school to plan INSET as well as to contribute to the LEA development plan.
- Experienced officers are prepared to share their skills in monitoring and evaluation with the school to improve the capacity of the school to engage in self-monitoring and self-evaluation.
- Any differences in purpose between internal self-monitoring/self-evaluation and monitoring/evaluation by officers are clear and openly acknowledged.
- Performance indicators and inspection criteria used by the LEA are made public and open to discussion.
- There is a shared agreement that monitoring and evaluation is in part about accountability (to governors, the LEA) and in part about helping the school to improve itself.
- Officers use the outcomes of all kinds of monitoring and evaluation to improve the quality of support they provide for the school.
- 'Quality assurance' is used to celebrate and publicize the school's achievements and strengths.

Resource File 5:

Co-ordinating School and LEA Planning Cycles

As a development plan provides a comprehensive and co-ordinated approach to *all* aspects of planning, it is to the mutual advantage of governors, head, staff and the LEA to work together to create planning cycles which are, as far as possible, compatible and convenient.

Working together to plan coherently requires:

- building a shared understanding of the role of the development plan in the work of the governors, head, staff and the LEA;

- clarifying the constraints on planning that exist;

- identifying all planning activities currently taking place.

There are *school* cycles (e.g. staffing, curriculum, finance, assessment; meetings of the governing body, parents, staff); *LEA* cycles (e.g. returns to the LEA, education committee meetings); *DES* planning demands (e.g. GEST bids, the annual curriculum return, consultation meetings); as well as *school–LEA interdependent* cycles (e.g. finance, inspection and monitoring, GEST, INSET).

Co-ordinating these various planning cycles:

- maximizes the efficient use of time and resources;

- provides coherence to the work of the school and LEA;

- ensures that appropriate INSET is available to support professional development.

Meshing the school development planning cycle – which in theory can begin at any time of the year – with other planning demands is easier when governors, staff, head and LEA officers undertake a *joint* mapping exercise. The purpose of such an exercise is to identify the optimum timing for the school development planning cycle so that all aspects of planning are integrated and co-ordinated.

A STRATEGY FOR MAPPING AND CO-ORDINATING PLANNING CYCLES

The following strategy is useful for mapping planning issues within the school as well as between the school and the LEA.

131

Step 1

A list is prepared of all the issues which have an impact on the planning process: What is needed, when and by whom?

Step 2

The list is then divided into those issues which occur at fixed points in the year and those for which the timing is more flexible.

Step 3

Fixed points are taken first and the issues are then mapped out using some flexible method (e.g. a felt board, cards and pins / flip chart, cards and Blu-Tack). Points of conflict are thus highlighted and compromises will need to be reached before proceeding.

Step 4

Once fixed points are mapped, issues with more flexible timing are added and distributed through the year to spread the workload and to provide the best fit with fixed points.

Some people find it easier to do this mapping exercise using concentric rings to represent the annual cycle. However, there is a problem in that cycles sometimes overlap. Others prefer to map in a longitudinal way which allows for such overlap. Figures 1 and 2 illustrate these approaches. In practice, some schools find a shorter cycle than a year preferable; others have a fifteen-month cycle with a third term of implementation overlapping with a term of audit and construction for the next cycle. Yet another variation is to plan two terms of implementation followed by one term of review.

As school and LEA practice and terminology vary considerably (e.g. for internal planning cycles, in the timing of financial information, in the allocation of GEST funding, in the role of the development plan in relation to the monitoring and inspection policy), the figures are provided only in outline.

The head, governors, senior staff and officers will decide how best to co-ordinate the different planning cycles and demands on the basis of the planning processes and procedures in their school and LEA. The advantage of such a joint approach is that planning becomes more co-ordinated and integrated to the mutual benefit of all involved.

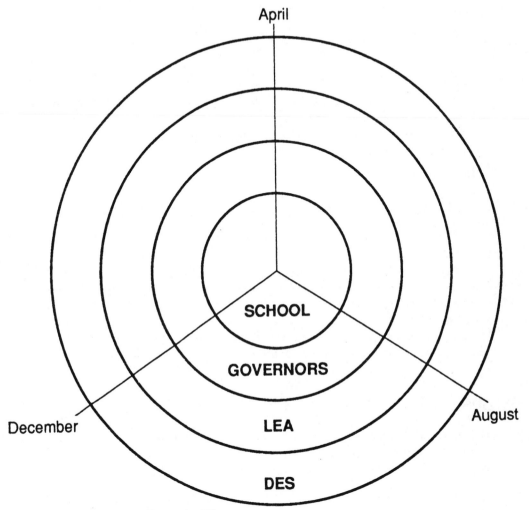

Figure 1 *Mapping planning cycles (1)*

	YEAR 1 Spring	YEAR 1 Summer	YEAR 2 Autumn	YEAR 2 Spring	YEAR 2 Summer	YEAR 3 Autumn
School						
Governors						
LEA						
DES						

Figure 2 *Mapping planning cycles (2)*

Resource File 6:

Working out Relationships between Governors, Head and Staff

The role of the governing body continues to develop as governors assume their new responsibilities. Each governing body will decide for itself how it should be involved. At one extreme, they may devolve almost everything to the head and the teachers. At the other extreme, they could be so involved that they confuse their responsibility for broad policies and finance with the role of the head and staff in being responsible for running the school. Neither extreme is desirable.

It is important for governors to remember that however keenly they may feel about particular priorities for development, the active support of staff is required if development is to be successful. This means that at various points there will need to be open discussion among governors, head and staff (and perhaps sometimes with parents and pupils) to ensure shared understandings about development planning, a clarification about respective roles and responsibilities, and a common commitment to improving the quality of education provided for pupils. There are a number of ways of doing this:

- The chair of governors and the head deliberately place educational issues on the agenda of governors' meetings in order to keep governors abreast of current debates.

- Agendas and briefing papers are prepared in jargon-free language.

- New governors who may be unfamiliar to the school are allocated mentors, another governor and member of staff, who are responsible for their induction.

- Governors are 'linked' to curriculum leaders and heads of department.

- Governors are regularly involved with staff and the local community in discussions on the mission of the school.

The following further advice draws from experience in many schools on how governors might best be involved in development planning.

Governors can make an important contribution to a review of the school's strengths and weaknesses. They should comment on what they see as the strengths of the school, for this helps the school to take pride in its achievements, making it easier to face the challenge of undertaking new developments. Governors are also aware of weaknesses, especially those identified by parents and the local community. If these are shared frankly with the head and staff, with the aim of making the school a better place for both teachers and pupils, then these can usefully be set alongside the staff's own perceptions.

In the light of the information arising out of the audit, and in the knowledge of the demands coming from national and LEA policies, governors will form views about which aspects of change should become priorities for development in the first and in subsequent years. The head will also be searching for agreement about priorities among the staff, who may have different views about what the school should tackle first.

In all schools there should be procedures for discussion and consultation about priorities. It is the head's job to prepare a draft development plan for discussion by the governors. Once the plan is approved, the head will lead the staff in turning the plan into a series of action plans, which guide the staff in the process of implementation.

It is, of course, for the head and staff to put the plan into practice. The extent to which governors may be involved in implementation depends on the priorities chosen. In some cases it may not be appropriate to involve governors very much. In others, they have a great contribution to make. Examples would be: improving the school's links with local industry and commerce; improving the liaison between teachers and parents; improving the school's image in the local community; and organizing resources for some aspects of the school's work.

Other examples are less obvious. A governor from industry might be able to improve the staff development in the school by providing a link with management training in a local firm. A governor from the world of commerce might be able to help with financial planning. Governors may be able to help check local and parental reactions to some of the changes made as part of the plan, or give advice on how to record progress with particular priorities.

Governors will particularly need to know about the outcomes of the plan and the views of the head and staff on possible priorities for the following year's plan in the light of:

- their experiences so far;
- the changing needs and circumstances of the school;
- new external demands and pressures.

Wherever possible, governors should see for themselves the changes and improvements in the life and work of the school which have arisen directly from the implementation of the plan. In this way they can both help to put the plan into practice and increase their involvement in the school in practical ways.

Resource File 7:

Collaboration and Teamwork

Governors, heads and staff have all reported how development planning encourages collaboration, and how this makes implementing the plan both more enjoyable and more effective. The school's partners often want to help but do not know how to do so: development planning provides genuine opportunities for harnessing this goodwill and support.

Collaboration:

- creates a commitment to a common purpose among governors, head and staff and the school's partners;
- improves communication and reduces misunderstanding;
- fosters creativity in finding solutions when problems are discussed;
- enhances motivation;
- prevents individuals from becoming isolated;
- generates a sense of collective achievement;
- supports teamwork.

Teamwork leads to better decisions and speedier completion of work through the pooling of expertise and the sharing of tasks. The team leader has a key role in managing the work of the team and in promoting a team spirit.

Teams are working well when:

- members are clear what needs to be done, the time-scale involved and who is to do what;
- members feel they have a unique contribution to make to the work of the team;
- mutual respect prevails among members;
- a climate of trust encourages the free expression of ideas, suggestions, doubts, reservations and fears;
- individual talents and skills are used effectively;
- members are able to discuss alternative approaches and solutions before taking decisions;
- there are established ways of working together which are supportive and efficient in the use of time;
- progress is checked regularly and members are clear about who they report to and when.

Resource File 8:

Devising a Staff Development Policy Linking Individual to Institutional Development

Until recent times few schools have had written policies for staff development, or a co-ordinator (or committee) with responsibility for its planning and evaluation. Previous policy has tended to focus on the professional development of *individual* teachers attending INSET courses by choice.

The weaknesses of such an approach are:

- staff receive inadequate advice on their professional development;

- INSET is a matter of individual choice, so some staff get much and some get little or none;

- professional development and INSET is often not related to the needs of the school;

- most INSET takes place outside the school;

- the outcomes and gains of individual professional development are not necessarily shared within the school.

The growth in school-focused and school-based staff development, the existence of professional training days, and the experience of appraisal schemes are beginning to lead to better policy and practice for staff development. Development planning builds upon this trend in the following ways:

- The plan focuses on the school's needs and the professional development required to meet these needs.

- Appraisal schemes provide links between individual needs and those of the school as a whole.

- Every teacher is seen to have rights to professional development so there is a more equitable distribution of opportunities for INSET.

- Since professional development is directed to the support of teachers working on agreed topics (the targets and tasks), the knowledge and skills acquired through INSET are put to immediate use in the interest of the school.

- Staff who undertake INSET have a framework for disseminating their new knowledge and skill.

- There is improvement in the design and use of professional training days.

- Information on external courses is collated and checked for relevance to the school's needs.

- School-based INSET and external courses are used to complement one another.

- Staff development is included in the school's budget.

Resource File 9:

Success Criteria and Performance Indicators

Both success criteria and performance indicators are new names for old and familiar processes.

A *performance indicator* is a qualitative or quantitative measure for judging the performance of an individual, group, institution or system.

For example, a pupil's GCSE result is the measure of his or her performance in a subject. If the GCSE results are collated, they can be used (in raw or adjusted form) to judge the performance of a class, school or nation and then compared with the performance of other classes, schools or nations or with previous performances.

Headteachers have for many years reported to governors on the work and progress of a school and presented evidence for it in terms which can now be called performance indicators – pupil achievements and results, attendance, attitudes and behaviour, the quality of relationships, extra-curricular activities and special events. In the same way, the reports or reviews of inspectors/advisers are replete with performance indicators.

A *success criterion* is a form of performance indicator. Success criteria are distinctive in that they:

- refer to future rather than past performance;

- relate to a planned target designed to improve performance;

- are chosen by the persons who set the target;

- influence the way the target is designed;

- emphasize success rather than failure;

- are a key component of each stage of development planning.

These six characteristics of success criteria are shared by some, but by no means all, performance indicators.

In recent years there has been considerable discussion of performance indicators in education. Different groups and agencies have produced lists of possible performance indicators. There has also been wide discussion of the problems of devising and using performance indicators – reliability and validity, fairness and credibility, value and justification.

Performance indicators operate at three levels:

- *The school*, by which the school judges its own performance.

- *The LEA*, by which the LEA judges its own performance, or the performance and curriculum provision of its educational institutions as a whole, or of a single institution (e.g. by inspection).

- *The national bodies* (such as the DES or HMI), by which a whole system is judged.

In devising success criteria for targets in a development plan, a school may draw upon the wide range of performance indicators developed at each of these three levels. A school may also use evidence of performance indicators collected at each level to shape its own priorities and targets. For example, the annual report of HM Senior Chief Inspector, a TVEI Review report or an LEA report on its own work can be used as sources of *standards* (against which the school compares its own performance) and of *ideas* (for audit or development).

Performance indicators and success criteria are seen by many to be important because of their relevance to the accountability of schools (how 'outsiders' judge their quality) and to the improvement of schools (how 'insiders' plan development). These two functions can be in tension: greater accountability does not automatically lead to improvement and vice versa. Of equal importance is the way performance indicators and success criteria can exert a positive influence on *ways of thinking* and *ways of working* in that they:

- promote desirable goals for schools;

- suggest standards appropriate to such goals;

- guide the action needed to achieve agreed standards;

- distinguish between process and outcome;

- indicate the evidence needed to judge success;

- help in reporting success;

- shape further action if the degree of success falls short of expectation.

When these basic ideas permeate ways of thinking and working, the process of development planning is enhanced.

Resource File 10:

Annotated Bibliography

One of the purposes of Chapter 14 is to locate our approach to school development planning within the context of the research literature on school effectiveness and school improvement. Development planning is also related to a number of other topics which have their own literature. Some readers who wish to explore these issues in more depth, however, may well find the wealth of literature available a little daunting. We have therefore provided this annotated bibliography on books related to school development planning which in our opinion provide a useful introduction and overview of their respective areas.

EDUCATIONAL CHANGE
Fullan, M. (1991) *The New Meaning of Educational Change*. London: Cassell.

An extremely comprehensive review of the change literature that is at the same time analytical and critical, practical and theoretical. It provides common-sense advice on coping with the ironies, paradoxes and complexity of living through the change process in schools.

SCHOOL EFFECTIVENESS
Mortimore, P., Sammons, P., Stoll, L., Lewis, D. and Ecob, R. (1988) *School Matters*. London: Open Books.
Rutter, M., Maughan, B., Mortimore, P. and Ouston, J. (1979) *Fifteen Thousand Hours*. London: Open Books.

These are the classic texts on school effectiveness in the UK. As they contain full descriptions of large-scale research studies, practitioners are advised to read them selectively.

SCHOOL IMPROVEMENT
Hopkins, D. (ed.) (1987) *Improving the Quality of Schooling*. Lewes: Falmer Press.

The International School Improvement Project produced some fifteen books, but because they are published in Belgium they are sometimes difficult to obtain. This book presents an overview of ISIP from a UK perspective.

Joyce, B., Hersh, R. and McKibbin, M. (1983) *The Structure of School Improvement*. New York: Longman.

This is an unusual book because it contains a detailed and accessible account of the 'what' and the 'how' of school improvement. Innovations that support improvement are described within a framework for implementation and cultural change.

Louis, K. S. and Miles, M. (1990) *Improving the Urban High School*. New York: Teachers College Press.

Case studies of five inner-city high schools during the process of improvement. They provide the basis of a state-of-the-art analysis of how to 'turn around' large and difficult schools.

SCHOOL MANAGEMENT
Caldwell, B. and Spinks, J. (1988) *The Self-Managing School*. Lewes: Falmer Press.

Written for schools who are facing the challenges of devolved funding and increased responsibility, this book is a combination of academic and practical advice. It is the book responsible for the proliferation of 'one-page policies'.

Handy, C. and Aitken, R. (1986) *Understanding Schools as Organisations*. London: Penguin Books.

Well known for his writing on management, Handy teams up in this volume with Aitken (a CEO) to apply his theories to education. In a very challenging book they discuss the differences and similarities between schools and businesses, the role of individuals and how schools can respond to and manage change.

Hoyle, E. (1986) *The Politics of School Management*. London: Hodder and Stoughton.

This short and readable book provides not only an overview of traditional management theory, but also an introduction to newer concepts such as 'micro-politics' and 'symbols'.

Hoyle, E. and McMahon, A. (eds) (1986) *The Management of Schools* (World Yearbook of Education). London: Kogan Page.

Contains a series of commissioned articles on a wide range of educational management topics. Its comprehensive scope makes it an excellent introductory resource.

Peters, T. (1987) *Thriving on Chaos*. London: Macmillan.

The most popular writer on recent approaches to management offers a punchy discussion of customer responsiveness, fast-paced innovation, empowerment and leadership. Not directly about education, it is however full of challenges, provocations and suggestions for heads and senior staff.

LOCAL MANAGEMENT OF SCHOOLS
Davies, B. and Braund, C. (1989) *Local Management of Schools: An Introduction for Teachers, Governors and Parents*. Plymouth: Northcote House.

This brief introduction focuses on the management of delegated school budgets, which are explained in simple terms.

Hill, D., Oakley Smith, B. and Spinks, J. (1990) *Local Management of Schools*.
   London: Paul Chapman.

A brief introduction with background material on the Education Reform Act and
developments in other countries. The management of the delegated budget is not
treated in detail, but the topic is set within its wider context. Useful chapters on
monitoring and evaluation and on changing roles and responsibilities.

TEACHER APPRAISAL

Bollington, R., Hopkins, D. and West, M. (1990) *An Introduction to Teacher Appraisal*. London: Cassell.

The authors were members of the School Teacher Appraisal Pilot Evaluation team,
and through a review of the literature and their experience on the evaluation, they
provide advice on planning and implementing appraisal schemes. A sustained argument is made for regarding appraisal as a fundamental component of teacher and
school development.

Evans, A. and Tomlinson, J. (eds) (1989) *Teacher Appraisal: A Nationwide Approach*.
   London: Jessica Kingsley.

This book contains a comprehensive series of articles on teacher appraisal; many of
the contributors were involved with the national pilot scheme.

CHANGE STRATEGIES

Abbott, R. *et al*. (1988) *GRIDS School Handbooks*, 2nd edition, Primary and Secondary versions. York: Longman for the SCDC.

This is the revised version of the widely used practical handbooks on school self-
evaluation. The GRIDS approach is flexible enough to be used with a wide range of
review criteria, and can be easily adapted for school development planning.

Schmuck, R. and Runkel, P. (1985) *The Handbook of Organisational Development in
   Schools*. Palo Alto, CA: Mayfield.

An authoritative, comprehensive and practical guide to the activities and strategies
that can assist in building a capacity for managing change at the school level.

Name Index

(box) after a location reference denotes a box in the text.

Subject Index

(fig) after a location reference denotes a figure in the text.